TEACH THE

WHOLE
PRESCHOOLER

D1429924

TEACH THE

WHOLE PRESCHOOLER

Strategies for Nurturing Developing Minds

CINDY TEREBUSH

W.W. Norton & Company

Independent Publishers Since 1923

New York • London

Teach The Whole Preschooler
Strategies for Nurturing Developing Minds
Cindy Terebush
Copyright © 2017 by Cindy Terebush
Interior photos by Steven D. Katz

For information about permission to reproduce selections from this book,
write to Permissions,
W. W. Norton & Company, Inc.
500 Fifth Avenue
New York, NY 10110

For information about special discounts for bulk purchases,
please contact W. W. Norton
Special Sales at specialsales@wwnorton.com or 800-233-4830

Manufacturing by LSC Harrisonburg
Book design by Molly Heron
Production manager: Christine Critelli

Library of Congress Cataloging-in-Publication Data

ISBN: 978-0-393-71154-7 (pbk.)

W. W. Norton & Company, Inc.
500 Fifth Avenue
New York, N.Y. 10110
www.wwnorton.com

W. W. Norton & Company Ltd.,
15 Carlisle Street, London W1D 3BS

1 2 3 4 5 6 7 8 9 0

Note to Readers
Models and/or techniques described in this volume are illustrative
or are included for general informational purposes only;
neither the publisher nor the author(s) can guarantee the efficacy
or appropriateness of any particular recommendation
in every circumstance.

Dedicated to
Michael Terebush and Scott Terebush,
who make me proud to be called Mom
and
Todd Terebush,
for whom mere words cannot express
my gratitude and love.
Everyone should have a partner
as supportive as you.

CONTENTS

INTRODUCTION

I was sitting in a hotel lobby when I received an email from Deborah Malmud, a vice-president at W.W. Norton & Company, Inc. and the editorial director of the professional books division. She asked if I'd ever considered putting my talks in a book format. I blog. I write articles for other venues, and yes, I had considered it, but I certainly didn't have a manuscript yet. After I spoke with Deborah, I began a process that I knew would be a pivotal time in my professional life. I had grown accustomed to standing in front of audiences, but now I had an opportunity to reach so many more people. I spent a lot of time thinking about the message that I want to share about what is good and right for young children and the impact of this unique opportunity. I knew it would be a daunting task and was slightly tempted to shy away from it, but when doors open I do believe in walking through them. What did I want to say in the 50,000 words or more that make a book, and how did I want to say it?

I have a pile of books next to my nightstand that are partially read. I started some but didn't feel compelled to keep reading them. Life distracted me and that was fine. I wasn't drawn in. Some were simply facts with no personality. Others were not relatable. I knew that I wanted to write a book that would be read from beginning to end. I thought about the feedback that I receive after speaking engagements. Many people comment that I am relatable, funny, and that they enjoy learning through stories that are part of the common experience of teaching in an early childhood setting. I have been told that both my presentations and my blog teach without criticizing. I knew that I wanted my book to be all of that. I want teachers to pick up this book and know that it is written by someone who understands them—who is one of them. All of us, children and adults, learn more when we find the task to be enjoyable. As you read this book, I hope you nod at the familiar and laugh with the irony of human behavior. I hope that you turn a page and think, "Hmm. I hadn't thought about that situation that way before so I should think about that." More than anything, I hope you remember.

Remember childhood. Remember sitting on a swing with the warm summer sun on your skin as you developed gross motor skills and coordination by pumping your legs back and forth. Remember when your biggest responsibility was to put your toys away. Remember endless days playing with neighborhood children who also shared your journey to school and days in classrooms. Remember the teachers with whom you felt a connection and the kindness they offered you.

I ask adults to remember childhood and they tell tales of hours playing in their neighborhoods, going to playgrounds and exploring. Children need to play, explore, and discover how to survive in the world so they will be able to be independent of their parents. We know that their adults impact how they view the world and how they view themselves.

I say these things in front of audiences large and small, in filled classrooms, ballrooms, and lecture halls. Everyone nods. There is inevitably agreement, and yet the room is filled with people who want to hear that message. In the beginning of my speaking career, I wondered why the rooms filled if the educators already knew what I was saying to be true. I wondered why I filled rooms with people who seemed to already know what I was saying.

I started to pay a lot of attention to the evaluations that I received after conferences. Some conferences share the actual forms with presenters, and others send a summary. I know that filling out evaluation forms isn't a favorite activity at conferences, but for a presenter they are an important professional growth and learning tool. I read the comments so I can learn what audiences hear when they listen to me. I want to know if teachers learn something that they can take right to their classrooms or if they do not. By reading those comments, I have learned that teachers have not forgotten how young children learn. They simply feel stuck in a system that is speeding out of control on a road of unrealistic expectations and they don't know how to stop it.

This book will not teach you how to stop the runaway expectations. We cannot control that. We cannot stop parents from being afraid and worrying about their children's success in today's world. We cannot stop governments from enacting educational policies that are contradictory to what is good for children. Over time, I hope that they understand from you and from people like me that they are on the wrong path, but we cannot put a screeching halt to it.

This book is about appropriate expectations of young children and so it has to model appropriate expectations of adults. It is not an immediate solution being published to end what we cannot end. It was written to teach and affirm appropriate expectations and to give educators ideas how to do what is right with the children in their care. This book is to help you to teach by controlling what you can—yourself and your classroom environment.

It is not possible to turn back the clock to a time that we remember fondly. If that were possible, every generation would have gone back. My parents were nostalgic about the 1950s, and their parents lamented the end of the 1920s. They couldn't go back and neither can we. We can, however, learn effective ways to forge forward.

Effective educators spend their time trying to connect their students to new concepts through meaningful and impactful interactions. We care about process, brain development, and thinking skills. In every generation, the teachers' biggest challenge is to take the information to the students rather than expect the students to come to us anxiously ready to receive all that we know. The adults have to go to the children. We have to go to the world in which they reside. Children now and forevermore reside in an instant information, highly paced, always connected world that revolves around consistently fed fears. It is so different than it was merely one generation ago.

A moment ago, I invited you to remember. Now I ask you to accept. Accept that those times when children roamed neighborhoods freely are all but gone. Accept that the world has become more competitive and it is possible that dreams can be harder to attain. Accept the increases we see in the number of students with special needs. Accept that children today know no different, and so they can actually be happy and be taught in a developmentally appropriate manner within the confines of current trends. Accept that you can make a difference by being an intentional teacher who questions current constructs and is willing to change.

This book will guide you through considering your routines, approaches, actions, and reactions. We will consider the whole child. Our students are not only vessels for information. They are emotional human beings with newly emerging socialization skills and cognitive abilities who need to figure out their world. They need to be the doers, and we need to help them to expand their thinking about themselves and the world. You will learn how to approach learning experiences with thoughtful consideration and you will be given strategies for updating your interactions and lessons.

Change is not easy but it can be so worthwhile. As you read, you will see the commonality of our work while you consider your individual practices. We are fortunate to live in a time when we know more about how children think, learn, and develop their sense of self. All this knowledge should encourage us to ask ourselves the difficult questions:

- Why am I doing the activities that I do, and are they meaningful?
- Am I doing everything possible to form a positive foundation for the students?
- Do I need to let the ideas from the past go in order to make room for new approaches?

It is important to develop partnerships with parents. Beginning with Chapter 2, each chapter ends with Quick Notes for you and discussion points for your communication with parents. Those chapters include information and ideas that can be brought directly to your work with young children. The Quick Notes will allow you to refer back for quick reminders of what was in the chapter. The discussion points will help you to share information with parents about how their children think and learn so they understand that even with today's pressures, their children can be taught with developmentally appropriate lessons that reflect our knowledge that they are whole people. Our expectations and the expectations of their parents need to foster a positive sense of self and a love of learning. We need to help parents to balance with us in the middle of today's Expectation Tightrope.

TEACH THE
WHOLE
PRESCHOOLER

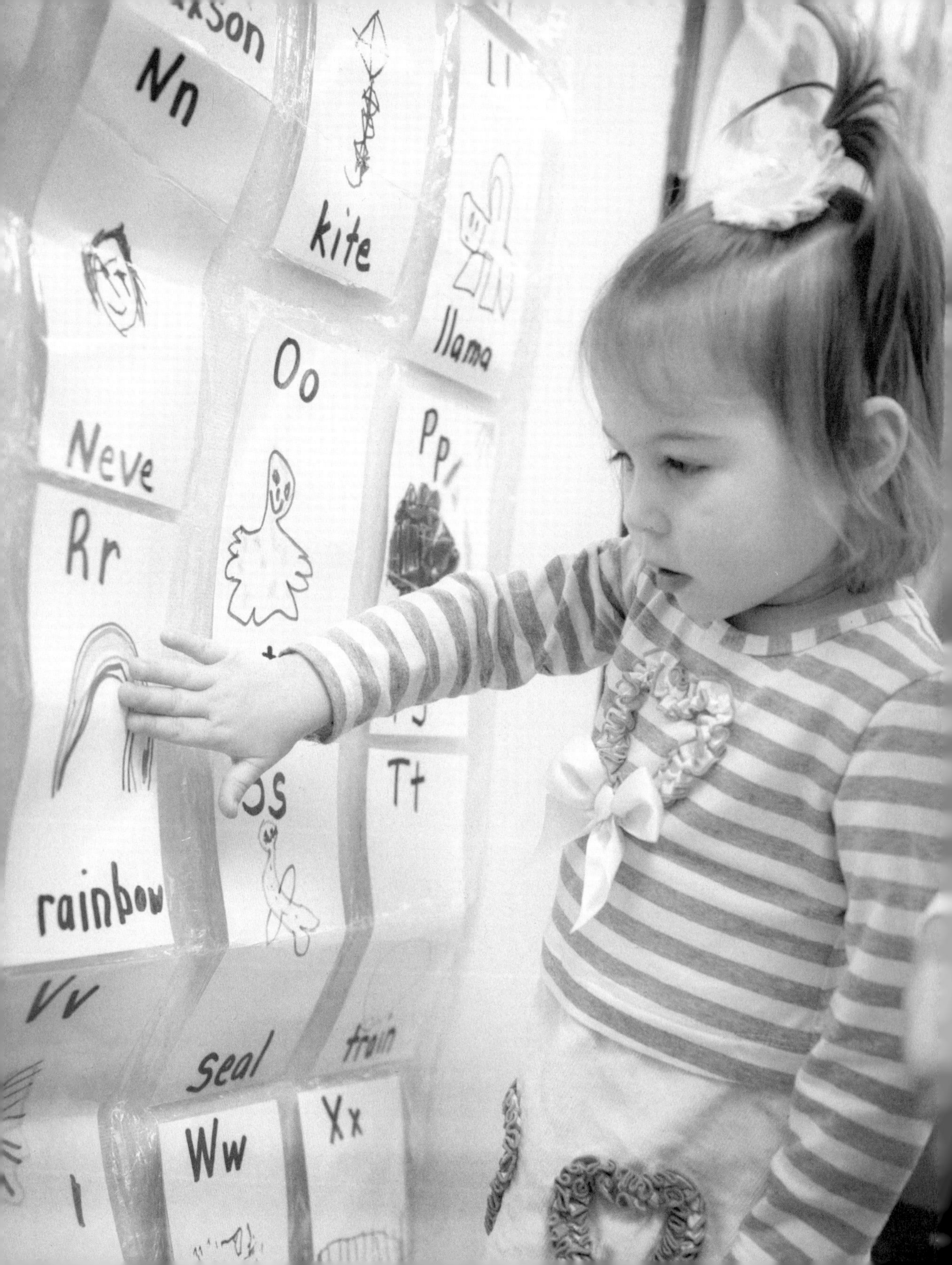
Nn
kite
llama
Oo
Neve
Pp
Rr
rainbow
Tt
Vv
seal
train
Ww
Xx

CHAPTER **1**

The Expectation Tightrope

It was a typical first day of preschool. Strangers were being brought to a strange land, and each one reacted differently.

Amanda bolted out of her car and jumped up and down as her mother worked to get her baby brother from the car seat. She couldn't wait to get into the building. Her older sisters went to school and she'd always wanted to go there. She had friends who went to that magical, big girl place before her but her mother kept saying, "When you are four years old . . ." Amanda was sure it would be a place full of friends like the ones her sisters brought home. She was sure she would get homework and that's important business. She heard crying and saw a little boy who was sad. She shrugged. She finally got to go to school.

"Joey, you're going to have fun," his mother begged as she picked him up. Joey didn't want to go into this strange building. It was scary. Anything could happen and it was too scary. It was making his stomach feel funny and he thought that terrible throw-up thing was going to happen, so that made it even more terrible. Joey thought his mommy knew he was having the jumpy tummy and she didn't care because she carried him in, saying,

"You are three years old, Joey. You are a big boy." He thought, "No. I want my mommy," as a stranger reached over and took him from her arms.

Julie and Suzanne saw puddles and ran for them while their mother yelled, "Stop! You're going to get all wet!" They didn't care about wet. They didn't care about this place called school. They were used to mom yelling to them. At four years old, the twins already knew there was power in numbers. Grownups yelled a lot. They could do anything as long as they were together. They could run when people said to walk. They could let go of a grownup's hand in the street. They could throw and hit and all that would happen is yelling.

Mrs. Jackson welcomed Amanda, Joey, and the identical twins, whom she hoped she would be able to tell apart soon. She knew that they all had much to learn—socialization, appropriate behavior, self-worth, academics, and how to become a whole class. The twins ran into the room and were throwing sand from the sand table. Joey was still in her arms crying. Amanda was looking so much less confident than she did in the parking lot. Every year Mrs. Jackson wondered how long it would take for them to function as part of a group. Just as she got to the sand table to talk to the twins, another child arrived and wept by the doorway.

The preschool classroom is typically the first place in which children encounter institutional expectations. It is where they need to figure out how to manage independently in a world full of the unknown without their most trusted adults. The young children, developing at different rates and from different family settings, are asked to join with a community of strangers and become one unit of alphabet reciting, song singing, easel painting skill developers. Preschool educators have themes, lesson plans, and curricular goals. They have expectations for each age group with the end goal being readiness for the next year. In the early childhood years, which span infancy to third grade, development is such an individual journey that group expectations become a delicate balancing act. That balancing act has little to do with specific skill achievement. It is a tightrope that determines how our goals will impact each child's self-image, confidence, and will to discover new things.

When I began my career in early childhood education, children were not asked to trace and write the alphabet as young as they are today. They weren't expected to "race to the top." We were told that tracing the alphabet and identifying letters was a skill that was taught midway through the pre-kindergarten year. We were not permitted to teach it to younger children. It bothered me every time I had to discourage or nearly ignore the children's attempts at a skill that was designated for the following year. When children are developmentally ready to try a new skill, they will ask to do it. Children on the advanced end of the developmental bell curve but not yet in the pre-kindergarten class would often ask their teachers to help them write letters. They would make attempts on their own and look for adult approval by saying, "Look at my A," or "Did I do this right?" We were permitted to tell the students that they wrote well but were not permitted to extend their curiosity by introducing new letters or their sounds. I often wondered whether we would know the children's true potential and how, by not offering more information, we were discouraging their explorations.

Times have definitely changed during the course of my 20 years of working with children. These changes have made me rethink my approaches to teaching young children. The children are growing up, it seems, in an entirely different world with different advantages as well as different pressures. If so much has changed, then how can we possibly say, "I've always done it this way, and so be it"? This book is the product of the observations I've made of both the changes in our world and the children's reactions to us as early childhood educators. It has emerged from my many years of working with young children and from my own questioning of practices that have been virtually unchanged for years.

Consider the differences between now and as little as 20 years ago. We have entered an age of immediate information and connection, increased competition, and worry. Our approaches to early childhood education need to reflect the times in which our students are living.

Technology has become an everyday part of our lives. The expectation that adults will consistently be available, answering email, and addressing matters of business has somehow bled into our expectations of children. Early learners, like adults, have business to attend to and have schedules that rival the busiest executive's. The children have things to achieve that require more time at desks and less time at play. They run from preschool to playdates and gymnastics or martial arts or dance. They have people to impress and places to go. Participating in activities for fun seems to be becoming a thing of the past. The children train from young ages to be on the elite team, the travel team, or in the competition group. The expectations of today's youth are focused on products and not process. Schools are emphasizing the importance of standardized test results at younger ages. Parents tell me about appointments for interviews and assessments for their children entering public school kindergartens. The pressure is on, but process still matters. Growing and developing skills is a process. Developing a positive sense of self is a process. As you will read, both require our thoughtful consideration of how we speak with, guide, and teach our youth.

There seems to be so much comparing and competing even outside the classroom setting. Human beings are animals born with the instinct to survive. Survival of the fittest used to mean surviving among the other animals. Now, it means getting to the top of the class and knowing more than the person next to you. It means performing better so that someday you will be a success. That need to be the best is fed by an increased awareness of the lifestyles and achievements of others. Social media has become an integral part of most people's lives. The children are growing up in a world with less privacy. Adults are more aware of the activities of other families than they were when sharing the day's activities required a phone call or handwritten letter. Even the children are more aware. They will tell me that their neighbor goes to dance or their friends took pictures on a boat. In my experience, young children are more keenly aware than we even realize of the comings and goings of the people around them. They need us to teach them from a very early age that they are capable and they should celebrate their own efforts.

When you really know people, you understand that all of our lives have ups and downs. We all sometimes experience success and failure. It is hard to remember this when we are being bombarded by social media posts. On social media, most of the pictures we post are of successes. Families are gathered at celebrations of children's achievements, and we can watch the festivities via pictures posted on social media. We read about other people's children who won awards or earned stellar grades. It tugs at our adult insecurities. We don't mean to do harm by trying to figure out where our family members are in this technologically depicted food chain. We are worried. Will our children be able to keep up? Will they emerge victorious in our society's version of survival of the fittest?

A byproduct of living in a world in which everything is available immediately is that we have lost an ability to wait for nature, for the natural development that happens over time. The change in availability of what we want in relation to the speed at which we can obtain it is also evident on social media. Consider the "selfie." Only a couple of hundred years ago, to have your likeness you would have had to sit for a portrait. That took time and effort. There were many hours of sitting as a painter meticulously created a painted copy of you. Then, film was invented. People didn't need to sit as long, but there was a wait for the film to be developed. Now we can take photos with our smartphones and, voilà, instant image. The technology has been changed and rewired so that our images are immediately available. We cannot, however, make development of the human brain happen at a faster speed. That "technology"—the wiring of the brain and the way in which it develops—has not changed. Children still develop each in their own way and at their own speed much as they did hundreds of years ago when people had the patience to sit for those painstakingly painted portraits. Parents are used to fast. Even children are used to fast production. They become frustrated with their own need to learn one skill at a time, and they want to be able to master new skills quickly.

Young children, barely verbal two-year-olds, know that information is instant. I was talking to a group of children in a two-year-old class. They asked what kangaroos eat. I wasn't sure and didn't want to give incorrect information, so I told them that I didn't know and would find out. A two-year-old looked at me and said, "Look on your phone. Your phone tells you." The young girl knew that the knowledge of the world was at my fingertips, or more precisely was in my pocket, and there was no reason to wait for an answer to their question. Young children and their parents are far less used to waiting for answers and products than in generations past. It is no wonder that they want to see evidence that their children are learning and will read faster than it can actually happen. As early childhood educators, we need to have a firm understanding of the development of these skills and the tools with which to teach parents about the process. Parents want to help their children to achieve, and this book will help us to more clearly define achievement and the steps to get to our goals.

It is becoming more commonplace for parents of typically developing preschoolers to express concern that their three- or four-year-old children are not writing yet. Often, children of that age are not even showing an interest in writing. I explain to parents that literacy skills include more than just writing. The children may be speaking well and enjoying books. They can tell us about stories that we read to them and participate in activities and games that encourage them to make up their own stories. Children may have vivid imaginations and fine motor skills that are on par with others their age, but just not be ready to decode written language. I assure concerned parents that an interest in reading and writing will come.

We try writing in sand and salt to see if multisensory activities are more appealing. Paper may not interest them yet. I remind parents that, like some adults, their children may always prefer auditory activities rather than visual. The students need time, and we need to observe their development. More than once this has elicited a response like, "But my friend's child can write. She takes pictures of what she writes and posts them all the time. My child needs to write."

This adult expectation is about fear and not facts. There is a pervasive fear today that children will not be able to keep up, pass tests, and be in the advanced classes. We are mistaking evidence of knowledge with particular products. Many people are not valuing the process of considering, evaluating, and developing critical thinking skills as much as they value the product that students produce from that process. The real learning that will sustain the preschoolers cannot be seen on paper. It is evidenced by their ability to reason. We need to be guardians of the process, but to be effective we need to consider our approaches with individual students and the activities that we introduce.

Students are increasingly expected to produce knowledge on pieces of paper as evidence that they are learning and will be ready for the pressure-filled years ahead. Early learners spend less time freely playing and more time at lessons run by adults with an agenda. Several years ago, a group of students in the school I directed were enrolled in drama classes. The parents of these three- and four-year-olds told me how much I would love what they were doing because they were acting and pretending. I sighed and pointed out that they were participating in someone else's pretend. The teacher at the drama lessons told them what to pretend. That is not the same as spending time creating a world of their own making and exploring the roles of the characters who would live there. It does not nurture their decision-making skills or explorations of socialization. In these pages, you will get a chance to consider the importance of self-expression both during play and through children's own creations. You will consider child-driven lessons as a way to help them become critical thinkers.

I recently was listening to an audiobook that asked a great question—in fact the book is called *A More Beautiful Question: The Power of Inquiry to Spark Breakthrough Ideas.* I often listen to nonfiction audiobooks when I take a walk, and this one stopped me in my tracks. Author Warren Berger asked that we consider how many facts children really need to memorize and spit back at us in an age when facts are at our fingertips. He asked if, instead, children should be learning to question rather than answer (Berger, 2014, pp. 47–50). I stopped the audio and thought, "Oh my gosh. There it is. It is at the heart of what doesn't feel right about this constant back-and-forth that starts in early childhood classrooms, even in this era." Adults teach a fact, ask a question, and need the correct answer. There is so much more to navigating the world. I agree so wholeheartedly with Berger. If a two-year-old knew that the answer to a question was in my phone, why are we spending so much time on things that will not help them as they get older? When they want to know a fact, they will reach for technology. When they need to work on a long-term project or solve problems so that they reach their potential, will we have taught them to do that?

Years ago, I wondered how children who were not challenged could reach their full potential. If adults did not offer them the opportunity to try new skills that were assumed to be for chronologically older children, how would any of us know their real capabilities? Today, I wonder how our ever-changing and increasingly pressure-filled world will discourage children from having a love of learning and confidence in their own abilities. I wonder if we are ensuring that we teach the lessons that will give them a positive self-image, decision-making abilities, and the character to keep trying when they experience less than stellar results from their attempts.

At first glance, the expectation tightrope seems to have the levels of academic expectation at each end. To the left of the tightrope would be a label that reads: "low expectations." They may be happily playing and discovering but there is no encouragement to go further. There is no one trying to extend their thinking because there are no expectations that their learning can be deepened. They do not know the feeling of attempting, deciding, and doing more than they thought possible. They play with the toys, get bored, and walk away. Adults do not watch and attempt to ask questions that would prompt the children to consider the toy from a different point of view. No one questions. No one ponders. There seems to be nothing new to explore. There is a rigid endpoint to the skills the children are allowed to attempt. In contrast, the label at the right end of the tightrope would read: "unreachable expectations." Children would never quite reach a point at which they felt triumphant. They would forever be reaching for what they cannot developmentally achieve with success. They may be able to attempt skills, but the result would not ever be good enough for the adults who are evaluating their progress. They discover at a very young age that they cannot meet the demands of the adults. They are defeated before they have really begun.

When early learners attempt new skills, they look to us for clues as to their success. Young children will attempt to trace a letter or paint a new picture, and they glance over to see if we are watching and smiling. They begin to feel worthy when we, as their role models, smile and say, "That is a great painting," or "Good letter writing!" They smile and continue to paint, write, and hone their new skills.

I cringe when I see young children try so hard to master a skill, and adults critique rather than encourage it. At four years old, a child who is able to write words with little assistance is mastering skills that many children at the same age cannot. Instead of celebrating that ability, adults will look and say, "The second letter of the word shouldn't be uppercase, honey." The four-year-old will learn that as he continues to master the skill of putting oral communication in writing. Celebrate the accomplishment now. At another time, when the child isn't investing his whole ego into showing you what he can do, point out that words are mostly comprised of lowercase letters. Point it out when the child isn't writing at all. When he is reading a book, say: "Look, did you see? Most letters are lowercase." Let the children feel success whenever you can. They need to know the joy of it so they will want to feel it again as their skills are built one upon the other.

The two ends of the tightrope are not as simple as "We don't expect you to master any skills," and "You cannot master these skills." The ends are really not about specific skills at all. Behind the façade of skill development lies the real issue. Our expectations impact every child's sense of self. At each end of the tightrope are the extremes of self-worth.

I remember when I understood this most clearly. I was tutoring a fifth-grader. She processed information differently than other students her age, and that made traditional classroom settings a challenging environment for her. As I got to know her, I realized that her thoughts were actually quite often far ahead of the average student of her age. She would shout out questions in rapid succession because she was ahead in the conversation and not behind. Unfortunately for her, traditional settings often do not allow for rapid-fire brain work. For years, adults had been trying to get her to stop and listen. She really was listening, but wasn't in the moment with the rest of us. One day, this fifth-grader turned to me and said, "I don't know why you try to help me. I am unteachable." I was aghast. Nothing could be further from the truth. I wondered where she even heard the word "unteachable." It is not a word that children use about themselves without having heard it elsewhere. This beautiful, intelligent young girl had spent so much time hitting an unrealistic expectation wall for so long that she didn't know why I would spend time with her. The educational world had failed her. It is my belief that the open-minded consideration of our practices helps us to lift children rather than defeat them.

This book can help to fire your thinking about the Expectation Tightrope, and where your methodology and approaches put you on the continuum of positive development to the less desirable negative messages that children receive.

In reality, this Expectation Tightrope has always existed. Educators have always tried to find the middle of the rope. They have tried to find that sweet spot in the center where there is perfect balance. We have always wanted to help children learn new things in a nurturing and developmentally appropriate environment. The challenge before us is not in changing our attitude toward the teaching of children but in accepting the changes in our world. We need to adapt in a way that prepares children for this society, not a society that existed when Head Start became the first publicly funded preschool program in the 1960s ("History of Preschool in the United States | K12 Academics," n.d.).

Walk into the typical preschool classroom, and you will find an interesting mix of activities that have never changed alongside computers, smartboards, and curriculum material that used to be taught to older children. It is as if an airplane flew overhead and dropped some technology and more advanced academics into the existing landscape. The items are placed in the space and used, but nothing in the existing structure has changed. There are activities that have been in early childhood classrooms forever and without question. They are sprinkled with the products of our changing world, and the two need to meld better.

The evolution of early childhood classrooms begins with acceptance. I lecture in rooms filled with teachers who remember a different childhood. Perhaps you remember a different time, too. Early childhood professionals and parents from my generation remember finger painting in kindergarten and learning to read beginning in first grade. They remember lazy days on the grass watching the clouds float by. They remember longer recess and days filled with play and pretend. They played sports for the fun of it and not to qualify for a showcase team. Their parents just wanted them to be able to go to school without crying. Pre-literacy skills weren't even a discussion in the preschool years. Today's adults wring their hands and worry about the effects of today's high-pressure world on tomorrow's adults. They wish it was the way it was when they were young. I wring my hands with you. I know, however, that we cannot go back. There has been too much forward motion. We have witnessed the rapidly growing technological age of the 20th and 21st centuries. Even those of us who didn't grow up with technology are hard pressed to imagine a world without smartphones, texting, and email. Though all that technology does not necessarily belong in an early learner's hands, it speaks to the world they will enter. We cannot ignore where their journey will take them. We cannot turn back the clocks and change the world back to what we remember and wish still existed.

In order to maintain a developmentally appropriate environment, we need to dissect, question, and evolve. We need to resolve the disconnect between how things have been done forever with the demands of the world that now exists. We do not need to replace all our existing constructs. We need to ensure that they provide the children with the foundation that they will need to succeed. Children need to develop their critical thinking skills and walk from their early childhood years with confidence in their abilities. We need to do what we do with more thought and reflection. We need to do what we ask of our students. We need to explore more and think deeper about what we do in our classrooms.

We are fortunate to teach a generation that can benefit from the findings of great theorists. Jean Piaget's Theory of Cognitive Development helps to define the stages of learning that we see naturally emerge during the childhood years. The youngest children, to approximately two years old, are in the sensorimotor stage. They are learning to understand the world through coordinating their senses. We know from Piaget that not only do they need multisensory stimulation but that they actually have to do that which they are so often told isn't acceptable. Children in the sensorimotor stage have to employ all their senses, which means they do have to taste everything. The young child's propensity for putting everything in their mouth is actually a part of normal development, and we learned from Piaget that we need to allow for it. We also learned that when our early learners begin to pretend at about the age of two years old, they are entering the pre-operational stage. In both this stage and the prior sensorimotor stage, Piaget maintained that the children are egocentric and can only see the world through their own needs, wants, and opinions. Spend one day in a preschool classroom and you will see endless evidence of this egocentric world view. Every cry of "That's mine!" or "I want it!" and every lack of developmental ability to show empathy and cooperate supports the notion that children throughout the early childhood years see the world egocentrically, with themselves as the center and as the only one who matters. It is, though, in the pre-operational years, which span from approximately two to seven years old, that we see the most language development and the important role that pretend play has in development of not only literacy but of the whole cognitive, social, and behavioral child (Lillard, et al., 2012).

Lev Vygotsky studied development and the possible impact of society and socialization on that progress. Unlike Piaget, Vygotsky believed that learning can lead to development and that a child's social and cultural experiences impact the way in which the child learns and grows. Vygotsky also taught a theory that is the core of what we now know about how to best approach learning in early childhood. He taught that children function at a higher level when engaged in play, particularly dramatic play (Bodrova, Germeroth, & Leong, 2013). There is so much evidence in our classrooms that the children are better able to focus and control behavior when they are at play. Young children can spend endless hours in their world of superheroes, princes, princesses, toy trains, and dolls. I have repeatedly seen three-year-olds negotiate the roles and rules in their pretend play, without adult intervention. It should come as no surprise because even as adults we are at our best when we are actively engaged in the learning environment. When I was a freshman in college, I was required to take a class about Shakespeare. As is the luck of most freshmen, I ended up in this class at 9:00 a.m. I was prepared to be miserable and to struggle to understand the material. Instead, I had one of the best educational experiences of my life. The professor came in each day and staged plays starring himself and a bunch of college students who initially didn't want to be there. He was great at making Shakespeare come to life in a way that we found to be fun and playful. Before long, it was a favorite class for many of us, and we had to admit that we understood what was happening in the Shakespearean plays. If adults learn so well when we are engaged in play and fun, then surely children do too.

We are also fortunate to have the theories of Erik Erikson (1950). His Psychosocial Stages of Development help us to understand how young children develop hope, will, purpose, and competency. At each age throughout our childhoods and adulthoods, Erikson claimed that our identity is formed based on particular struggles. Young children struggle with trust vs. mistrust, autonomy vs. shame and doubt, and initiative vs. guilt. It was Erikson's theories that helped educators to see that we must allow children to try what they are curious about and to do what they are capable of so they will be confident and willing to learn. It is based on Erikson's theories that I advise parents to let children feed themselves, even when it is messy. I tell cringing parents to let their children pick out and wear the mismatched outfits. By allowing them the right to decide and to do, we teach the children that they are capable. Erikson taught us the value of the right messages for development of self-worth. His theories should inform our practices about acknowledging effort and allowing for individual abilities. A child who is forming a healthy identity will learn that he/she can be autonomous and capable, can create by making good decisions, and will develop confidence in his or her ability to navigate the world.

We have made small strides with the knowledge of theorists of the 20th century. We prepare lesson plans based on the ages and stages in our classrooms. We try to remember to reward acceptable behavior. We encourage children to try new things. We study developmentally appropriate practice, which is based on the knowledge that all children develop at different rates. We need to take this knowledge further in the 21st century and beyond.

The foundation for future success is directly related to our position on the Expectation Tightrope. Children who feel capable and confident are more apt to take on new challenges willingly. Children who feel defeated and believe learning is a chore will not look forward to participating in new learning activities. One main goal of a preschool should be to send children forth with a foundation of confidence and a willingness to explore their curiosity. When they are confident, they will try. When I am confident, I will try. It is no different for children or adults. I remember sitting in chemistry class and feeling very lost. I wasn't the best math student, and I went in knowing that chemistry required math skills. I was hesitant from the start and saw every new bit of information as impossible to learn. Think about situations that you have experienced when you seem to never quite get it right. It is frustrating. If you can't get the tennis ball over the net and the instructor keeps telling you to adjust this way and that way, chances are that you will eventually stop taking tennis lessons. Adults say that children are resilient. Because they say that, we have a perception that they will always bounce back. We see them fall, get up, and continue running down the hall. We think, "I would still be on the ground assessing for broken bones." We cannot forget that the ability to bounce back from a fall is not the same as bouncing back from feeling incapable at a young age. Feeling incapable becomes part of our view of self and could take years to prove incorrect, if ever. Psychologists David Scott Yeager and Carol S. Dweck have studied students and resilience. They wrote: "Our research and that of our colleagues show that if students can be redirected to see intellectual ability as something that can be developed over time with effort, good strategies, and help from others, then they are more resilient when they encounter the rigorous learning opportunities presented to them" (Yeager and Dweck, p. 306).

Another primary goal of our preschools should be to develop critical thinking skills. Typically developing children will eventually write the letters and numbers. Not every young child is encouraged to reason, analyze, question, reflect, and evaluate. Young children want to know about cause and effect. They ask, "Why?" so often that adults begin to find it frustrating. We answer questions, give facts, and solve problems. We need to ask questions far more often than we do, and give young children the time they need to process and answer. We need to intentionally resist telling them how to complete tasks so they will get a desired result. We should ask how they think they should do it and let them try. Children want to be right. They have a desire to please when they are very young. A baby will repeatedly make the same sound if it makes adults react. Young children stand in the middle of a room and clap to get the adults to clap with them. They want an audience and constant congratulatory feedback. Young children need to learn to experiment. They need to experience the unexpected outcome and to learn that this is not always failure. They need to learn to accept that sometimes the experiment does not come out the way they wish and to consider what else they might try. Learning to identify where a mistake was made and how to correct it for a different outcome is a key foundational skill. Children who know they can make a mistake but may succeed when they try again will be more willing to attempt new skills.

Look around your classroom. Be mindful of the moments of your day. Consider the activities you offer and the methods by which you offer them. There are approaches, lessons, and methodology that you are doing just because they have always been done that way. That isn't good enough anymore. Every moment has to support a foundation of confidence, self-worth, and capability in an increasingly competitive world. Are you tired of the same songs? So are the children in your class. Do you have to consistently remind the class to pay attention? They aren't finding the activities offered to be compelling. Do you seem to be spending your days putting out fires and making corrections? If only one or two children are able to meet your expectations, you need to reflect and reconsider. Try one new methodology or change one activity at a time. Change is hard, and we make it seem daunting when we think that every activity and every one of our behaviors has to change at once. Try one new approach to an activity that you have been doing the same way for years. Give yourself an opportunity to be surprised by a positive change or to continue to experiment until you find what works for your students. Then remember that your students cannot change their behavior or abilities all at once either.

Step onto the Expectation Tightrope as we work to find new ways to approach preschool education and look for that place midway between lack of challenge and incapability. In that centered space, we need to change what we do to take today's stringent expectations and make them reachable for early learners. We need to know how the young children think and feel so we can offer a developmentally appropriate opportunity to learn and grow. Early learning is so much more than alphabet decoding. It is about a whole child who is growing socially, emotionally, and academically. The world is at their fingertips, and teachers need to be intentional when they plan experiences to explore.

A boy who just turned four years old walked over to a table where his classmates were tracing and writing their names. He picked up a pencil and scribbled over the preprinted letters of his own name. The teacher celebrated with him. It was the first time he found his name tag without help. It was the first day he wanted to write. The scribbling was a triumph. The opportunity was offered, and his progress was cause for joy. There were no limits to what he could attempt. His prior attempts weren't met with critique, and so, when he was developmentally ready, he bravely went over to the table to try. He was in a safe and nurturing learning environment. The rest would come.

CHAPTER **2**

What Do We Know About Young Children?

Jason was two years old and was a regular at our weekly class for young children and their adults. It didn't matter to us if children were accompanied by their parents, babysitters, or grandparents. Their important adult was more than welcome. Jason's mother worked full time so he attended with grandparents. One day, his mother was home from work and brought him to class. We were so excited for him. We thought that he must be excited, too, and wanted to acknowledge his special adult. Jason walked into the building holding his mother's hand. I said, "Jason, you have someone special with you today!" He smiled, lifted up his other hand and showed me his new toy train. He loved trains, and his focus was on his brand new toy. We assumed, as adults often do, that our thoughts match theirs. Their priorities are not our priorities. We are not that alike.

Young children are not small versions of adults. They do not see the world the same way that adults do. They are looking through a different lens with a different focus. We live in two entirely different spheres. When a young child walks over to you with a doll or a toy car and says, "Play with me," how do you feel? I ask this question frequently to groups of parents and educators. It is almost always met with silence. The attendees squirm. They don't want to say it. I offer, "Are you uncomfortable? Do you wonder how long this will go on?" They laugh and nod. When we play with children, we are pretending to pretend. We know it isn't genuine. We cannot go to that magical place anymore. Our "pretend" serves a very different purpose than that of a young child. Our pretend is about personal protection. We envision conversations that haven't happened yet. We imagine our reactions to others and to possible scenarios. Our thoughts try to prepare us for what may come and we try to imagine all the possible outcomes of our interactions and reactions. We know that reality is finite and we have prior experience with its limitations and possibilities. We see the world in a concrete, cause-and-effect way and children do not. We have become higher-level thinkers who have lost the ability to fantasize in the same way as our students.

In order to effectively plan learning environments for young children, we need to try to see the world through their eyes. We need to figure out how they think so we can appeal to their desire to know more.

Early learners are tiny in a world full of big. Everything towers over them. A group of adults is like a forest. Children cannot see their way out of a crowd. They are easily stepped on, tripped over, and overlooked. They need to look up to see the tops of tables. They cannot reach anything they need. They see the world from their own perspective without an understanding of their impact on others. Each of them assumes that we all see things the way that they do. This is their survival of the fittest.

"Mine!" children declare. If they want it, it must belong to them exclusively. I have often stood in a classroom and responded to the "Mine!" proclamation. I smile and say, "No. This is all mine and I let you play with it. This is my classroom and everything in it belongs to me. You can play with the toys. Isn't that nice?" This baffles young children. Everyone within earshot stops and looks at me. They seem unable to understand that everything could actually be mine. I watch as they consider this new information. It literally changes the dynamic in the room. They have to consider a possibility outside themselves. A young teacher once asked me if I thought saying that was a bit snarky. I told her that I wasn't being snarky. Instead, I have introduced the children to a new worldview, one which they had never before considered: Some things actually belong to other people, and it is nice of them when they share.

Jean Piaget, the developmental psychologist who developed the Stages of Cognitive Development, taught, "The egocentric child assumes that other people see, hear, and feel exactly the same as the child does" (McLeod, 2015). Early learners believe that if they want something, we must want them to have it. If they think something, everyone thinks it. They become frustrated when they want to play with a toy and we ask them to give it to someone else. It is a confusing situation for them. They cannot understand why we would expect something different from what they desire. They do not refuse to pass a toy to a classmate because they are being purposely oppositional. They simply do not understand a world in which their desire to keep it isn't paramount. This viewpoint of the world is a part of normal cognitive and emotional development. We cannot and should not attempt to undo it. The children will mature and develop a more empathetic, sympathetic, and larger worldview someday, but not today.

In preschool classrooms, we have 15 or more young children, each of whom sees him- or herself as the central and only important character in the action. We also have teachers with their own, very grown-up agendas. The children want to build with blocks, play dress-up, and put train tracks together. The teachers want them to learn the alphabet, count, trace lines, and master difficult tasks such as successfully cutting with scissors. The children develop at different rates and will all be ready at different times to read, write, and calculate. We are most ready to learn new information when we are motivated by our own curiosity. We must recognize that in order for lessons and experiences to lead to a desire for deeper exploration and learning, the concepts must matter to the children. The children will do what is important to them at the time. We need to make lessons appealing and intriguing.

Recently, I mentioned to a friend that I would love to have a bird feeder. I saw them at other people's homes and found watching the birds so peaceful. My friend had a hummingbird feeder in her yard, knew I would enjoy one of my own, and bought it for me. I was intrigued by how it attracted the birds. I read information on the Internet. My husband, who shopped with me for the nectar, was equally curious and did some reading. Both of us were amazed at the number of hummingbirds it attracted. We wanted to know why they were attracted to it, how they found it, and more! We had lived our whole lives not knowing that the color red attracted the hummingbirds and that their food was nectar, not seeds. We had no desire to learn about it before we received our hummingbird feeder and it actually attracted them. Suddenly, we couldn't get enough of this sort of information. Our curiosity had been piqued. An object that we put outside worked! It must be how young children feel when they build a ramp and a car rolls a long distance or they put the blocks in just the right balance so their castle freely stands. They cannot get enough. It piques their curiosity, and they want to do it over and over. They ask questions to figure out how they made this happen. They played a part in the activity so the details matter to them.

Observe adult behavior and you will see that we keep a piece of each stage of childhood with us. We can still be curious. We can find events miraculous. We keep tiny bits of that childhood, including the egocentrism. Think about your needs and reactions over the years. Have they really changed so much? When we are infants, we have a problem and we want it solved. Our diaper is dirty or we are hungry and we cannot wait. We cry louder and louder until someone comes. As adults, we don't necessarily weep louder and louder, but we do complain and want someone else to solve the problem. We are unhappy, tired, wishing for something different. We don't like the rules, so we make phone calls to institutions asking them to make us more comfortable. We remain just a bit egocentric, and it shows.

Often, we cannot understand why someone else is hurt by what we have done or said. We get frustrated when people disagree with our political opinions. Just like young children, we sometimes fail to see that other people can think differently, and that's acceptable. We also forget that in order for us to be engaged in an activity, we must have an investment. We have to find a movie interesting or we want our money back. We flip channels. We put books down and don't finish them. We hope that the person lecturing at our professional development class is someone we find to be relatable and funny. When we are bored, we tune out. The activity has to matter to us, too.

Why do we expect anything different from young children? If they don't care about what we are trying to teach, they will put it down and not want to finish. They will look around the room for something more interesting, just as we do when we don't find an activity interesting. When they are bored, we have missed the mark.

We have to be willing to abandon our neatly written plans that sounded like so much fun when we wrote them. If we are the only person in the room having fun, we have to admit that we have miscalculated. The topic has to matter to the child. The question becomes: Can you approach it so that it matters to the children? For them to attach to learning, it has to be about things, people, and experiences that they find intriguing. Find out what matters to them and tailor learning experiences to their interests—that is your mission.

In 1932, Piaget also wrote, "As long as the child remains egocentric, truth as such will fail to interest him and he will see no harm in transposing facts in accordance with his desires" (Piaget, 1997, p. 165). Additionally, Piaget theorized that until the age of approximately 12 years, children could not successfully separate fantasy from reality. Since that time, many researchers have observed and worked with children to try to determine their ability to separate fact from fiction. In 2004, for example, Sharon and Woolley postulated that children use their own experiences to determine what really exists and what does not (Sharon & Woolley, 2004, pp. 293–310).

The challenge, of course, is that they have such limited experience when they are young. Experiences also vary greatly from one child to another. A child who has never seen a zebra with his or her own eyes may decide that it is as much a fantasy as a unicorn. Children tend to err on the side of what they wish. Children who wish unicorns were real decide that they are real. Over the years, I have moderated many unicorn debates among young children. It seems that they readily believe in Santa Claus, the Easter Bunny, and the Tooth Fairy. Researchers have debated the notion that when their culture or parents support the belief that a fantasy is real, children will accept that fantasy as reality (Laking, 2001, p. 60). If their parents speak of the Tooth Fairy as a real figure and say that she leaves the money under their pillow, that imaginative figure may be accepted as real for far longer than their other imaginative play.

Just as each child develops motor and cognitive skills at different rates, each child finds the boundary between fantasy and reality at different times. When they are ready, they come to their trusted adults and ask, "Is the Tooth Fairy real?" Until they are ready to accept that this story may be fiction, they will not ask. There is not one specific day, month, or year when we can expect children to suddenly declare, "Now I know Santa and the Easter Bunny and superheroes aren't real." Those of us who work with young children have the privilege of watching that transition take place individually and in its own time for each child. We get to watch their brains begin to show signs of executive functioning when they can use reason to determine reality.

The majority of children in our preschool classrooms are still operating in a world where reality has no boundary and anything can happen.

They believe that superheroes can defeat the bad guys and that Santa Claus delivers presents on Christmas. Even children who don't celebrate that holiday may believe that Santa is real. As our Chanukah candles were lit, I remember my youngest sister telling us that she explained to a friend that Santa flies over our house and goes to the neighbors. She believed that Santa could be real, so she needed to fit our life without him into a paradigm that explained how he could exist, but not as a part of her specific experiences.

When you live in a world where anything can happen, it is difficult to accurately predict outcomes. If you cannot predict outcomes, then cause and effect will elude you. One of my favorite literacy activities with young children is when I ask them how they think a story will end. That usually has a few intriguing results. Some children leave the story entirely and just start talking about what they did with their families or friends recently. They are talking about what matters to them. Other children take the story to their favorite form of play. The story may have been about a dog on a rainy day but, in their prediction of the outcome, there are suddenly princesses and superheroes. Some children shrug. A few will declare, "The dog goes inside the house. The end." On occasion, a child who is more advanced at logical conclusions will make a plausible prediction. This activity is a good way to determine where children are on the fantasy-vs.-reality bell curve of development.

We expect so much from children whose worldview is not necessarily tied to reality. We want them to understand consequences in the real world, the world inhabited by adults. We want them to predict how we will react to their behavior. We want them to understand how their behavior impacts their classmates. Yet, most of us can name adults who don't understand how their behavior affects others. We know grownups who inaccurately predict consequences of their decisions. The young students in our classrooms are experimenting with a thought process that can elude even experienced adults. We need to remember that we work with children who believe that the monster under the bed can exist and that princes and princesses are real and live in castles. Oh wait—they are and they do. Princesses and princes do exist. We forget to help them make that distinction, too.

Adults are their truthkeepers. Children need to pretend and must be allowed to do so. When a child asks me if their friend who is dressed as a superhero can really zap them, I say, "That is pretend." When a child asks about Santa or the Tooth Fairy, I say, "You need to ask mommy and daddy." There are some truths that aren't ours to tell. At the same time, we need to be sure that our statements help children to see where the boundary of reality exists. That is how we teach cause and effect and right from wrong. As much as it is sweet and magical that children believe anything can happen, the ability to know the boundary between that pretend world and reality is an important skill.

Every interaction that we have with children shapes their worldview and their opinions of themselves. Developmental psychologist Erik Erikson wrote: "Children love and want to be loved and they very much prefer the joy of accomplishment to the triumph of hateful failure" (Waters, 2016, p. 3). We need to mind our interactions with children because we are their first mirrors. It is so hard to separate ourselves from the events of our own childhoods. Our sense of security begins there and follows us as we grow. Young children do something new or create something from nothing and look for our reactions. They want us to pay attention, and when we focus that attention on their good efforts, we teach them the feeling of accomplishment. When our attention is focused on what is wrong, we teach them to feel shame and doubt. One of the greatest gifts we can give to children in the early childhood years is the gift of confidence. When we are confident, we believe we can take on new challenges and learn new things. The acquisition of confidence needs to outweigh the teaching of specific academic skills in our preschool classrooms. We need to remind ourselves where our focus needs to be amid the demands for the perfect letter A or the introduction of sight words and math skills.

Have you worked for a boss who seems impossible to please? No matter what you do, it isn't done well enough. You try so hard and yet there is always something you can do better. It is defeating and affects your outlook on the entire experience. A young child attempts to trace a line and an adult walks over and says, "No, it needs to be on the line." The same young child tries to do a puzzle and an adult says, "Turn the piece. Wrong piece. Try that one." The child walks over to the clay and tries to make a snake. It breaks. Without being asked for help, the adult says, "Look. You do it like this." How many times in that day was that child wrong? As adults, we think we are helping. Often, we are being discouraging. As more demands for earlier learning of skills collide with children's developmental abilities, it becomes harder for them to master tasks and creates more opportunities for them to fall short of mastery and to feel that pervasive sense of failure and doubt in themselves.

In professional development classes, I often ask groups of teachers: "How often do you make children wrong?" They tell me that they do not. They don't use the word "wrong." They don't have to use the word to communicate the idea. Every time we say, "No, not like that," through our words or our actions, we chip away at a child's belief in his or her own capabilities. When a child is doing his or her best, the effort should be praised. The product will be honed with practice but only if the child is willing to keep trying. Celebrate the attempt and they will be more willing to try.

Adults also have a tendency to do things for children that they are capable of doing for themselves. As soon as children are able to walk, I ask their parents to stop carrying them into school. The message to the child who can walk but is carried everywhere is: "You do not do this well enough for me." Adults carry them because it is faster, takes less intention and time than slowing their own pace to match that of the child, and is easier than reminding them to hold hands. Swoop them up and it's done, but it gives the wrong message.

Teachers need to let children open their own lunches as soon as they learn how to do so. Show them how to open the bags and wrappings. Once they know how to open everything, it is imperative that there be enough time left in your busy school schedule to let them do it and to help them when they ask. Like every skill, managing packages with emerging fine and gross motor coordination requires time, practice, and assistance.

Resist making every decision for the students in your classroom. Confidence comes from knowing that you have decided upon actions that go well. They can learn to be confident decision makers if we let go of our need to be in control of every moment of every day. The children can decide what toys to play with and which books to read today.

We need to let go of control, starting with the most basic functions such as what food they will put in their mouths. Snacktime can be a time of choice. Much like carrying children who can walk, picking snacks for those who can talk sends the wrong message. Children have absolute control over two things—what food they swallow and if they will use the toilet. Children who feel less control in their lives will give adults a harder time with potty training and eating. We can help to give children a feeling of control over their lives by at least letting them choose the food they will eat. They don't need the choice at every meal, but snack is such an innocuous activity. The typical preschool snack does not require preparation and cooking. We reach for snack items that are already prepared and put them on the table. There is rarely only one item available in a school. Let them choose between two items. Confidence is gained through making good decisions and enjoying the outcome. For a child, selecting pretzels rather than crackers could be that good decision.

As the young children grow, they will gain skills. They will learn from trial and error. They will become developmentally ready to understand literacy concepts. They will absorb knowledge from the many forms of media that bombard them. Typically developing children will read, write, and count. I have had many students arrive at my preschool at the age of two or three years old reciting words from other languages that they saw on television or counting like people on TV. There are so many things that we have to admit that they can learn without classrooms. Piaget taught that all people go from being pre-operational to operational and formal executive thinkers. Their maturing abilities will emerge naturally but they will not gain confidence without our positive acknowledgment of their good works and deeds. It is our most awesome responsibility.

More than one teacher has asked me what to do when a child does, in fact, write something incorrectly or expresses frustration at the attempt. I remind them of the difference in their lives when they feel like someone is helping them or when they feel like someone is demeaning their efforts. When someone is helping, they ask, "Can I help you?" or they say, "I learned this," and they show you another way without drawing big, thick lines on what you've done. They show you another way to try, without making you feel unintelligent. We all want that respect from other people. We need to give that respect to children.

"Can I help you?" is such a simple sentence with so much power. The power is transferred from us to the children. Some children will give us permission to help. Others will say no. When they tell us not to help, we need to ask ourselves how imperative it is that this child master this skill today. Today, at this moment, can we let it go? Tomorrow is another day. Tomorrow, we can try another approach to introduce the activity. I often ask children who reject my attempt to help if they will come back later so I can show them another way to accomplish the task. Sometimes, the child is so frustrated that he or she instinctively knows that now isn't a good time to learn a different way. The child is too emotional. The child feels like the best thing to do is walk away. I have been known to leave my desk during a particularly frustrating task so I can take a breath and look at something new. I go back and try again. Giving a child permission to make that decision—I need to walk away right now—gives us the chance to teach that the task will be here waiting when you are ready.

Confidence comes not only from making those good decisions and having those decisions respected, but also knowing there is another chance. Asking children to try again can be an empowering activity. Try again and I am here to help you. I'm not going to demean you. I'm not going to make you feel incapable. I'm going to help you succeed, and success can take more than one try.

Perhaps we should stop thinking of young children merely as learners. The word "learners" implies that their role is simply to take in what others know. Their role is to discover, integrate, and expand upon that discovery. When we think of children as explorers who have the task of figuring out the world and how it works, our perspective on how to teach changes. Bernard Baruch famously said, "Millions saw the apple fall, but Newton asked why." I wish for my students that they feel safe and confident enough to be like Newton and freely ask why.

Their curiosity needs to be nurtured, but first, we need to be paying attention to what makes *them* curious and not what piques our adult curiosity. I might find a science experiment to be particularly intriguing, but if the children aren't paying attention then they clearly do not. The events that take place in my classroom and during the hours of my preschool should not be about me. The focus of the class needs to be about the children as explorers. We do need to introduce certain concepts, but we need to find where those concepts meet their curiosity.

A common springtime classroom activity is to watch caterpillars become butterflies. Year after year, schools order the kits and the caterpillars arrive. I go from school to school as a consultant and see them everywhere. I am always interested in the students' level of interest in what has become a preschool staple. In some classes, children can't wait to show me the butterflies. I am barely through the doorway when the children proclaim, "Look, Cindy!" and show me the current stage in the life of the butterfly. In other classes, no one points it out. I was in a class-room recently where the children were more excited about showing off their new shoes. I admired their shoes and then asked, "Do you have but-terflies?" A student in this pre-kindergarten class said, "Oh yeah. We had them last year, too." There was sort of a group shrug. Later, I asked the teacher if they had shown any interest in the caterpillars or butterflies since they were brought into the room. She said, "No. They aren't inter-ested," and shook her head.

I wondered out loud if they should try something else—another meta-morphosis—maybe ladybugs? I told the teacher that you can get ladybugs just as easily. She scrunched her nose and declared it creepy to have the bugs in the room. I suggested that it might reinvigorate an interest in nature and the changes in nature if the children never saw ladybugs develop. She rejected the notion. Obviously, her interest and comfort zone superseded the lesson about stages of metamorphosis. The lack of interest of her stu-dents wasn't going to change the lesson plan. The uninterested students weren't learning as much as they might have if the teacher had kept trying to find the activity that would appeal to their desire to know more.

There are times when we need to try another way, or even let the curriculum emerge from the students entirely. One day at lunchtime, a student was eating an apple that had been cut in quarters. He found a seed in the apple and asked us if we could use the seed to grow an apple tree. Whenever a student asks a question, we have a decision to make. We can just tell the facts as we know them, or we can find a way to let the students find the answer. In this case, we could have told the boy that we could not grow an apple tree. The conditions were not conducive to success. Instead, we told him that we would try to find out if we could get the seed to root.

By now, everyone at the table was paying attention to our conversation and everyone wanted to see the seed. We let them look at and touch the seed. We attached them to the activity through their senses. Then, we took the seed, wrapped it in a wet paper towel, and sealed it in a sandwich bag. We hung the bag in the window, knowing that it probably wouldn't work.

Later in the day, I spoke with the staff and we decided that we needed to expand their question by applying it to a different type of seed or bean that we knew would root. We needed them to discover that different seeds need different conditions. We had rooted lima beans before and knew that would work.

The next day, we brought lima beans into the classroom. We did not hold one up and say, "Look at the lima bean." We spread them on a table where, once again, the children's sensory curiosity could be piqued. They felt the lima beans. Some children sniffed them. As we talked about the beans, one of the teachers decided to cross the curriculum and have the students create a book in which they would record their findings. We involved children ages two to four years old in this experiment.

After the children interacted with the beans, the teacher asked them to describe the bean and draw it. Some children accurately made observations. They told their teacher, for example, that the bean was white or the bean was cold. Others were not as accurate. Younger children tended to say what they wished. One boy said that the bean was blue. Blue was his favorite color, so that wasn't a surprise. When he said that, the teacher wrote it. She took exact dictation. His statement didn't need to be accurate, and we didn't need to make him wrong.

The curriculum had been crossed from science to literacy—what you said is now written on this paper. After the teachers took dictation and the children drew, a number of lima beans were placed in a paper towel in a sandwich bag and hung in the window just like the apple seed from the day before. As we knew would happen, the apple seed did not change. It didn't grow roots or sprout in the bag, but the lima beans did. The children were excited when the lima beans sprouted and rooted.

The teachers took beans out every step of the way so the children could feel the roots and sprouts. They touched, smelled, and recorded their observations each time there was a new development in the growth of the lima bean plant. They enjoyed the literacy activity that became a part of the science experiment.

The staff had successfully taken a concept that the children were curious about and let them explore. They offered multiple opportunities for expanded learning. At the end of their lima bean explorations, I asked the students, "Were we able to grow an apple tree?" They replied, "No. The apple seed didn't do it but the beans did." They thoroughly enjoyed "The Seed Book" that they had created together, and asked throughout the year that we read it to them. So much learning would have been lost if we had simply said, "No, we cannot grow an apple tree in here."

Young children are explorers who are solving the problems of nature. A preschooler may spend endless weeks going back to the block area in your classroom. That preschooler is trying to solve a puzzle. The child cannot necessarily express to you the dilemma, but that doesn't mean there isn't one he or she is trying to solve. The child who favors the block area is curious about spatial relationships, weight, and balance. That is just as valid a curiosity as is expressed by children who favor the book area and want to decipher the words. We can try to encourage them to try new things, but we need to be sure to make it a puzzle—a curiosity that they can explore. When you are with children and you say, "Go try the blocks," it isn't nearly as intriguing to them as when you say, "There's a puzzle in the block area today. Can you help to try to figure out how to get them to balance as tall as you are?"

Young children, egocentric and trying to build confidence, are more apt to try new skills and expand their knowledge when the activities are about them. For years, preschool teachers have started word recognition with names. We want children to recognize their names but, more importantly, they care a great deal about their names. It is the first activity meant to encourage a love of words. Every skill needs to be approached in the same way.

We need to approach every new concept with a plan to tap into their natural curiosity through a methodology that centers the activity on their senses, their desire to explore, and their unique worldview. We need to look at the curricular requirements and decide not what day we will teach it but how we can encourage the children to care. We need to carefully define success in the early childhood years. If our students are explorers, and they naturally are, then success is a positive encouraging journey and not a product.

CHAPTER 2 QUICK NOTES

Young children are:

- Egocentric and see the world only from their own viewpoint.
- Struggling for power and seeking independence.
- Developing a sense of who they are and what they can do themselves.
- Learning to think critically, make decisions, and become part of a group.
- Unable to separate fantasy from reality.

Build independence and decision-making skills by allowing children to:

- Open their own lunches.
- Walk rather than be carried or put in a stroller all the time.
- Select the toys they will play with.
- Determine what center to go to.
- Pick the book to be read.
- Pick their own snack.
- Pick their own art materials.

Questions for children who are frustrated or struggling:

- Can I help you?
- Will you come back to try again later?

CONVERSATION POINTS WHEN COMMUNICATING WITH PARENTS

- Their children's curiosity is the doorway to more learning.
- Children need to explore in order to solve the puzzles of the world.
- Active, interested learners retain more new concepts.
- You cannot force children to be developmentally ready. Your role is to grasp their curiosity and add to their explorations.

It is important that parents learn about:

- The natural egocentrism of the early childhood learner. Explain that the children need to be interested and engaged for long-lasting, deeper learning to take place.
- The importance of fostering independence. It is in the early childhood years that children develop a sense of self (positive or negative) and we have to work to promote self-worth.
- When curiosity emerges, it is our role to grasp onto their exploratory nature and add to their knowledge.
- Remind parents that not everything needs to be mastered immediately. Learning everything is a process.

CHAPTER 3

Our Words Matter

Take a few moments to watch young children as they pretend. Put everything else away. Put down your pen and your lesson plans. Just watch and listen. The children in the dramatic play area are developing their language skills. They are negotiating as they each try to exert power. They are managing their social world.

Even children who pretend all by themselves use language. Verbal children talk to themselves with words that we recognize. Children who do not yet have words may imitate the tones and pitches of the language they hear around them. Typically developing children tend to incorporate sounds and words in their play. When they don't know the word for something, they might even make one up. It is through the natural act of pretend play that they begin to label their world. They use the words and phrases that their parents and teachers use. Watch, listen, and you will see it happening.

As they develop an understanding that words are symbols for everything around them and for everything that happens, children begin to think, express themselves, dream, and interpret events using vocabulary that they have learned from interactions with others. They are listening and imitating all the time. The precision with which we use words helps us both to understand nuances and to have others understand us. The words we use with and about the students in our classrooms matter a great deal. They are learning about the use of language from us in real time. Unfortunately, using words is so automatic for us that we often don't question our own application and usage.

Early childhood teachers spend a great deal of time ensuring that their classrooms are print rich. We ensure that books are available, and that there are words on every item. Look around and you see signs that say: "window," "table," "chair," and even "wall." We want children to associate the words they say with the printed word.

Part of the job of the preschool teacher is to teach vocabulary—even the bigger and harder words. Preschool teachers who do science experiments, for example, should teach words such as "condensation" and "metamorphosis." Using the correct terminology is simple when we are talking about words related to our curriculum. Determining vocabulary words for specific classroom experiences isn't nearly as challenging as giving consideration to the words we use in everyday conversation.

Our use of words needs to be accurate and precise. We often neglect to consider how our words can impact a child's experience both with peers and as self-worth is developing. Before we approach any other literacy lessons, we need to reflect on our use of language and be intentional in our speech. We need to be careful to use words accurately to both teach vocabulary and model consideration for use of language skills.

The word "friend," for example, has been misused in early childhood classrooms for decades. When we tell children that we are all friends and everyone in the class is your friend, we are not accurately stating the situation. Not all the children will be friends. You are not, after all, friends with everyone you meet. Some children will like each other more than they like others. When we tell them that they are all friends, we set them up to be confused and hurt. Eventually, usually in the pre-kindergarten year, one child will look at another and say, "You aren't invited to my birthday party," or "You can't come to my house." How crushing and confusing when we have purported that everyone is a friend! It is untrue and an unrealistic expectation that every child will enjoy the company of all the other children.

I remember being an elementary school student and being forced to play with the children of my parents' friends. Though I was young, I remember knowing that I didn't like these people. I didn't want to go their house and I especially didn't want to have them in my house touching my toys. Alas, I was young and had no choice.

It is often the plight of young children to be forced to spend time with people they don't really like or with whom they are uncomfortable. My parents were not going to give up their friends, and perhaps that wouldn't have been a reasonable request from an eight-year-old. To my parents' credit, I don't remember them calling these children my friends. I remember them telling me to be nice and suggesting that I might have fun. I think they knew that calling them my friends would be pushing it. In early childhood classrooms, we all too often push that word incorrectly.

The lesson that children need to learn in the early childhood years is that they get to pick friends, but there is a word for what they all are to each other. They are all classmates. Classmate is the appropriate word for use in school. The directive should be that the children are classmates who need to be kind to everyone.

We should be teaching kindness rather than friendship. The truth is that we cannot teach "friend." Each of us has different needs and tastes. We each have a different concept of the word "friend," especially in current times when friends may be people we've only met online and never in person. We can, however, teach kindness. Kindness is the long-term, universal goal. When a child says, "You cannot come to my party," the response should be about the importance of being kind. The lesson that young children should learn is that even when we don't particularly like someone—when we are not compatible—we still need to be kind. Wouldn't that be a nicer world for us all?

When we use the word "friend" so universally and insist that everyone has to be friends, we also go against their natural instinct to be selective. We are turning off a little bit of their self-protective intuition. Keep in mind that when they are teens, we will want them to discriminate between whom they should spend their time with and who may be less compatible. It is fine for them to start understanding compatibility and incompatibility in the early childhood years. They just need to be considerate of each other.

The children are also not the teacher's friend. For years, preschool teachers have referred to students as their friends. "Come with me, friends." They are not your friends. They are your students. They are your class. They aren't your pals.

For the same reason, I question the use of first names to address teachers. The children in preschool classrooms do not arrive at elementary school to an invitation to call their teachers by first name. There is no logical reason that they cannot be taught to address adults by last name. If they can say Ms. Veronica or Ms. Stephanie, they can say last names. I have asked teachers of different ages of early childhood learners why they think teachers use the term "friends" to address the class and their first names when children are under the age of five years old. The answer is always that it creates a warmer, friendlier environment. The environment is created by your actions and interactions. I have warm and nurturing relationships with students who know their general label is student rather than friend, and that I am Mrs. Terebush. To the children, the terms don't matter nearly as much as your approach and attitude.

Additionally, if we truly are tasked with preparing children for the elementary school years, we are making a mistake. We are not teaching the correct formalities when we teach young children to call us Miss

Cindy or Miss Mary. They will not go to kindergarten, first, and second grade and call their teachers by first name. I don't need to be called by my first name to have a caring relationship with my students. I can still be nurturing, warm, and respectful, and be Mrs. Terebush.

After getting used to using the words "classmates" and "students," consider what you call that gathering of children on the carpet. The phrase "circle time" intrigues me. Unless you are holding a circle, the directive, "Come to circle," is entirely inaccurate. We do hope they will sit in a shape that is circle-like, but their gathering is more accurately a meeting. Some schools have told me that they call it "morning meeting." Others call it "group meeting." Far too many schools are still calling it "circle time." The students actually react differently when they are called to a meeting. "Meeting" is a very adult word. Their parents talk about meetings they have attended at important places, such as work. Children at surprisingly young ages understand that a meeting is an important gathering to discuss pressing matters. When I've said to preschoolers, "It's time for our group meeting," I've had some of them tell me about their parents' meetings. I've had students tell me, "My mommy goes to meetings." Once, a young boy told me, "My mommy and daddy went to a meeting at my brother's school. It was big trouble!" I couldn't help but smile.

In my workplace, the phrase "group meeting" became just "group." Teachers would say, "Time for group," and parents in the hallway told me that it sounded like therapy. I responded, "Yes, it is like therapy. They will come together and talk." We laughed and I decided that the word "group" was still accurate. It had the correct meaning for the situation.

Now that we have accurately named our time with the entire class, consider a word that we overuse when the children are playing together. We stand across crowded rooms and say, "Share. You need to share that!" The children look at us perplexed and they carry on with their grabbing and complaining. They are perplexed, in part, because the word means nothing by itself. The meaning of the word is situation dependent. The word "share" does not describe what we want them to do and it is actually nearly impossible to accomplish at their egocentric age. In the early childhood years, it would be more accurate to use words that tell them exactly what we need them to do. We want them to pass the toy or take turns. It is possible for young children to pass a toy once they feel they have possessed it.

When people don't know the meaning of a word, we tend to infer it from the context or from our past experiences. The inferences that children make when we use the word "share" can cause a great deal of frustration. A young child's experiences could inform her that share means a variety of actions. In the past, the word "share" could have meant they had to give something to someone else. It also could have meant that the item suddenly became theirs for an extended period of time. A child who wants a toy from someone else might think that when you told a classmate to share, you meant "Give it to her now." The other child could believe that when you said to share, you meant "You can't have that anymore." Not only does the word "share" take on a negative, "You cannot have that anymore," connotation, but an adult's definition of the word is rarely the same twice in a row because the child's role in the scene is not always the same. The child can be the giver or receiver randomly. When we say, "Take turns," it means the same thing in every situation, no matter the current possessor of the toy. Give the children a directive that is clear, consistent, and possible for them to achieve.

Not only do our interactions with children need to be clearer, but our own actions and intentions need to be labeled accurately. The word "discipline," for example, has morphed in our everyday usage. "Someone needs to discipline that child," or "Don't they discipline those children?" are common phrases. Often, when people make those statements, they mean that the children need to be punished. Punishment and discipline are not synonymous. When we use the word "discipline" as a noun and ask people to name a discipline, they say that sports, martial arts, and other similar activities are disciplines. A discipline is an activity with a particular set of rules. Therefore, when we discipline children, we are actually teaching them a set of rules rather than punishing poor behavior choices.

Early learners need to gain an understanding of the different rules that may apply to them in the different places in their lives. There may be different rules at home than at school. There may be different rules at school than on their sports team. They can be said to have discipline when they can accurately apply the required rules to their current situation.

Punishment, on the other hand, is an attempt to stamp out a particular behavior. Early childhood teachers are not tasked with punishing children. We are tasked with teaching them. We teach them that they can run on the playground, but we prefer them to walk in the hallway. We teach them that when they hit someone with a block, it hurts the other person and is not kind. We are disciplining.

When we are more conscious of our own use of specific words, we are better able to elevate the vocabulary of our students. It is an outdated belief that simple words need to be used with young children. It is amazing what concepts they can understand and then use correctly when they are provided with consistent and accurate context.

The adult use of baby talk is ironic. We work to teach independence, but our speech often doesn't reflect that goal. From the time they are infants, children are working to develop language skills. In their first year, babies imitate us. They coo and babble as they mimic the different sounds they hear when we speak. It is from listening to us that they learn that spoken language has a rhythm and beat. Their cooing voices range from high to low pitched, just like ours. When we imitate their adorable noises, they are amused. It is a fun game, but shouldn't be the model that we use to converse with them. When we bring our knowledge and abilities down to the level of our students—when we oversimplify and fail to challenge their skills—we fail at the job of lifting them up. Adults can be fun and engaging, while still attempting to raise the level of communication.

I cringe when people talk to children only in puppet voices, high pitched and silly. The adults are not giving the children the chance to learn how to speak like adults or the credit for being intelligent enough to realize the different styles and contexts of communication.

We need to elevate the children's emotional vocabulary, too. In early childhood classrooms, we tend to use about five words to describe their emotions. We tell them that we see that they are *happy, sad, mad, scared,* or *surprised.* But there are so many more emotions and degrees of emotion! "Happy" is different than "joyful," which is different than "ecstatic." "Scared" is less than "terrified" and different than "anxious." Young children are in touch with their feelings more acutely than many adults. They simply lack the vocabulary. By the time we are adults, we have learned that bursting into tears in the middle of the supermarket because they don't have our favorite brand of string cheese is inappropriate. We have learned to stifle our feelings. Our students have not had to stand in a room full of people and smile at someone who has just annoyed them. Their emotions are genuine, full of life, and in the present moment. They also seem to be far more in touch with their bodies' reactions to emotions. When I ask groups of adults how they feel when they are in difficult situations, they use emotion words. They say, "I feel angry," or "I feel annoyed." When children are upset, they use body words. They say, "My stomach hurts," or "My head hurts." We should be using the most accurate words we can find to label the emotions and their bodies' reactions for them. From our use of vocabulary, our young students can learn that right now, right at this moment, they are feeling gleeful or exhilarated, angry or furious. The more emotions words we teach, the better they will be able to communicate their feelings to the adults in their world.

The most important word that we neglect to teach in the early childhood years takes many physical forms. Sometimes it looks like anger and at other times it looks like fear. When we look at the context in which their emotions are triggered, we discover that the primary emotion that triggers the anger and fear is actually frustration. The children, who think the whole world sees events from their individual points of view, get so easily frustrated. They want something and can't make it happen. Another child has a toy that they want and they cannot always get it immediately. An adult gives a directive and it wasn't the action the child had in mind. We are constantly telling children to come here or go there. I imagine this feels a bit like when I am at my desk, need to complete a task, and am constantly being interrupted by requests and events that, in my opinion, are unimportant. I keep losing my train of thought and I get frustrated. I stop answering the phone and close my office door. I take a deep breath and know that the work can be completed tomorrow if need be. The young students cannot hold their calls and shut the door. They cannot necessarily go back to the task tomorrow, because it will be cleaned up today. They really don't even understand the concept of tomorrow. With all our good intentions for moving through our day, we contribute to their frustration. They cannot tell us. They can't say, "Excuse me, but I am in the middle of this puzzle and need five more minutes," any more than they can always control their frustration enough to say, "Mrs. Terebush, she took my block and I'm upset." It isn't a realistic expectation that the emotional reaction will be tempered by simply knowing the word "frustrated." It is, however, a lesson in both emotional intelligence and literacy when we help children to differentiate between the feelings and therefore the definitions of anger, fear, and frustration.

Be aware of word usage in your classroom all the time, not just when you are addressing the children and helping them to understand their own feelings. For some reason, adults forget that children can hear us when we talk to each other. We are half a body length taller so we think sound waves don't travel down. How wrong we are! When you think children aren't listening, they are. They hear everything you say. They watch everything you do. They strive to be as big and powerful as the adults in their world so they repeat what you say, often with the same body position and inflection that you use. Be careful not to say derogatory things about people. Avoid gossip. You are their role model of appropriate speech and kindness.

Role modeling is not an easy task. It isn't even a phrase that some people like to use. I have written articles that refer to teachers as role models and I often use the phrase during presentations. I have actually had professionals tell me to take out that wording or to avoid saying it aloud. People are burdened by the notion, and it turns them off. When I address the topic of modeling kindness and avoiding gossip, people visibly cringe. Adults fall into patterns of unkindness. Making other people seem less adequate helps some adults to feel more worthy. Why do we expect any less of children? Their capacity for empathy is still developing and it is the adults' job to model what we hope they will become. It is daunting to purposely examine our own behavior and ask ourselves, "Is this what I want the children to become?" That should be the overriding question for all our approaches with children—our word usage, tone, and to whom and how our words are aimed.

We cannot look at young children and say, "We all need to be kind," and then practice lack of kindness. The children will repeat our words, tone, and attitudes. When I was young, many of my relatives were cigarette smokers. It was of their generation. They started smoking before all the warnings and before the word "cancer" was even spoken above a whisper. Hosts and guests on television shows and actors in movies smoked on screen. It was not only acceptable in their generation, it was considered elegant and very adult. My relatives, perhaps like yours, would be holding a cigarette while they told the children, "Don't smoke. It's a terrible habit." Gossip and hurtful speech may not be as tangible as a cigarette, but they are just as apparent to young students, who are watching everything the important adults do.

The children can hear you. Your words need to be kind, accurate, uplifting, meaningful, gentle, and to set the stage for success. Your words need to be teaching, modeling, and pointedly building vocabulary. "Is this what I want these children, my students, to become? Is this what I want them to take from me as they navigate the world?" Those are the words that should be in every teacher's reflections. They should be the basis for planning. Our words matter as much as any other lesson we intentionally teach in our classrooms.

CHAPTER 3 QUICK NOTES

We need to use more accurate vocabulary in our classrooms and lift the children's use of words. For example, we must teach more accurate and specific vocabulary rather than the word "friend."

- The children in a class are classmates.
- Children in your class are students.
- Children in a neighborhood are neighbors.
- Children at play are playmates.

Here's some more accurate vocabulary than "circle time."

- Group meeting time.
- Morning meeting
- Afternoon meeting.
- Group gathering.

Here's some more accurate vocabulary than "share."

- Take turns.
- Pass back and forth.

"Discipline" and "punish" are not synonyms. When you use the word "discipline," it means to teach a set of rules or boundaries for a particular skill. In our classrooms, when we discipline we teach the set of rules and boundaries by which children can succeed at socialization.

We do not use enough, or sufficiently accurate, emotion words in our interactions with children. Children need to learn degrees of emotion and words such as:

- Frustrated.
- Joyful.
- Ecstatic.
- Terrified.
- Shocked.
- Anxious.
- Gleeful.
- Exhilarated.
- Angry.
- Furious.

CONVERSATION POINTS WHEN COMMUNICATING WITH PARENTS

- We need to reinforce with parents the important role that they play in lifting their children's vocabulary and understanding of the world through their word usage. Assure parents that their children can learn without angst that the word "friend" should be reserved for actual friends, while others can be classmates, neighbors, even mommy's friends' children. Let the children begin to self-select their definition of a friend.

- Parents also need to know that their expectation that young children can successfully share may not be developmentally possible, so they need to be specific with phrases such as "take turns."

• Remind parents that children with impressive vocabularies have
  been spoken to by people who are precise in their word usage
  and who do not bring their vocabulary down to the level of very
  young children. They know that the children can learn more
  complex words.

Teach parents that coping skills begin with the ability to accurately label
emotions. They need to use a variety of emotion words to give names to
the feelings of their children.

CHAPTER **4**

Play Doesn't Mean Only Dress-Up

One of my favorite quotes comes from Fred Rogers of *Mr. Rogers' Neighborhood*. He said, "Play is often talked about as if it were a relief from serious learning. But for children play is serious learning. Play is really the work of childhood" (12 Life Lessons from Mister Rogers, n.d.).

Early childhood classrooms are filled with toys. Actually, if you filled the room with empty boxes, the children would still build, create, and play. The plethora of colorful toys feels like our nod to play as an important activity. Even in an empty room, children will run, chase each other, and create pretend worlds. They would be mommies and daddies and superheroes. They have vivid imaginations and they have the puzzles of the universe to solve. They require very few props because play comes naturally to them. Play isn't defined by the particular items being used. It is defined by the level of fun and brain stimulation as the child explores, experiments, and adds to previously obtained knowledge.

The National Institute for Play has identified seven categories of play: attunement play, object play, body play and movement, social play, imaginative and pretend play, creative play, and storytelling-narrative play

(Pattern of Play—National Institute for Play, n.d.). The categories include all the activities that children participate in with joy throughout the day. Play is not restricted to your dramatic play area or block center or train table. Play includes attunement or being in harmony with others, gross motor activities, socialization, creativity, and storytelling. It is the thread that ties together literacy, cognitive abilities, and motor skills. It is every-thing that humans need to experience to build a foundation for future learning, self-confidence, socialization, and emotional health.

Unfortunately, the erroneous distinction between engaging in intellec-tual pursuits and engaging in play begins with early childhood educators. They call children to tables to do crafts or literacy and math activities. When they are done, the students are often told to "Go play." Even though the teacher may understand that children learn as they pretend or build, giving the directive "Go play," sends the message that play happens apart from learning. Teachers send a message that what is happening at the table with the pencils or during their group meeting time is the serious business of learning. Teachers set up an environment with the message that there are lessons to be completed and, when that has been accom-plished, students are released from the chair and can go have fun. When we consider that play is any activity that is engaging to the children and promotes brain development, the directive to leave the table with the pencils and markers and "go play" is the wrong command. It would be more accurate to say, "If you are done at the table, you can find another fun activity in the room," or simply "What would you like to do next?"

Any activity can be fun, and every activity should be approached with the question, "How can I make this engaging for the children?" The ego-centric minds in your classroom will grasp onto any activity that they find to be joyful and that they feel they can achieve. If the activity matters to them, they will be curious and want to participate.

We do not easily retain information that isn't relevant to us. This is true for all of us. Four years ago, I attended my eldest son's college orientation. My son was living at college, so sessions about commuters did not matter to me. I tuned out. I started making a list of errands for the next day in my head. I didn't even realize when the topic had changed. We shouldn't expect any different from the children in our classrooms. If they are not engaged and the subject doesn't seem to matter to them, they will go through the motions while wishing they were by the dollhouse or toy car track.

Teachers need to respect the power of play and the children's capacity to build upon their own knowledge base—to scaffold learning. Give students the freedom of self-discovery by waiting for them to invite you into their play. Adults can ruin the best learning opportunities. When a group of children have negotiated the rules of play in the kitchen area and are happily using the pots, pans, and oven, adults walk over and ask for food. An adult will say, "Can I have a piece of pie?" when perhaps the children were making pizza. When we do that, many children will suddenly switch the game and agree to give us what we have asked for. The adult has ruined the original game—the activity that was born from the children's curiosity. The pizza making has ended. We will never know what puzzle about the world the children may have been solving by pretending to be the pizza maker in the neighborhood.

Another group of children are building with blocks. An adult sits down on the floor uninvited and starts building. The children will inevitably stop creating their structure and look at yours. They will contribute to yours or try to imitate it. In the meantime, their original building, which was an amazing feat of weight and balance experimentation, is abandoned.

Instead, wait to be invited to play. If the children want your input, they will extend the invitation. The children in the kitchen area will ask you what you would like to eat. The children in the block center will ask you to join with them or will hand a block to you. The children trying to make balls out of clay will hand you a piece.

The invitation to play allows children to experiment with decision making and power. They get to decide if you join with them. They get to decide the rules of the game. One former student of mine loved to play in a fast food stand that was in the classroom. The stand not only looked like a fast food counter but it made the sounds of one, too. He couldn't get enough of it. I would often sit nearby to see if he would invite me to play, and he always did. The scenario always played out the same way. He would ask what I wanted to eat. I would order a typical fast food option—chicken nuggets, fries, burgers—and no matter what I ordered, he would go to the stand, come back and declare, "We don't have any."

"Can I have chicken nuggets, please?" I asked every time.

"We don't have any."

"Can I have fries, please?"

"We don't have any."

It would go on and on. It was his way of refusing me in a socially acceptable format—the world of pretend play. Finally, I would ask, "What do you have?"

He always said, "Peaches." It was not typical fast food fare but it was his game, he invited me, and he got to set the rules.

I said, "Great! I would like some peaches, please."

He would go to the stand and return with the same news every time, "We are out of peaches." That always signaled the end of my participation in the scene. He handed out the final refusal and would turn to his classmates. I did not attempt to call him back.

If the children invite you, stay only as long as you are welcome. If they do not invite you, you need to accept that they do not want your input. It's a blow to the adult ego but it's the truth. They are fine without you and, in fact, are learning a great deal on their own. Resist the urge to insert yourself.

When you are not invited to play, spend the time listening to and observing the class as they freely participate in activities in the room. We can learn so much about how each child sees the world if we really pay attention to what they do and say while at play. A group of children were playing in my classroom and assigning the typical roles. The boy who seemed to be the leader of the group declared that he would be the daddy. One of the girls was assigned the role of mommy. There were a couple of babies in this pretend family and the rest of the children were the cat, dog, and bird. When the young boy had finished casting the characters, he said, "Okay, let's go over there. That's the house."

He walked over to a corner of the classroom with his family members. As soon as they started to play, he walked to the opposite corner of the room. The other children were confused and called him back. He went back but when the action began again, he retreated to the opposite corner.

One child asked, "Where are you going?"

He said, "I'm going to work. Daddies are gone all day."

By observing and listening, we learned about this child's perception of a father's role in a family. He has learned from his own life experience this version of the concept of "daddy."

The children who were cast as the dog and cat were gleefully crawling around the room. The sights and sounds of pretend domesticated animals are common in early childhood classrooms. Children get down on all fours and scurry around panting and begging. Teachers are putting out craft materials, trying to address an argument over a toy, and calculating the best time for snack. Suddenly, they are surrounded by young children with their tongues wagging in the air. Please stop what you are doing and pet the children. They are trying to figure out how it feels to be as powerful as the dogs and cats in their lives. That need for understanding of animals is not less important than tracing a line at your table.

If we acknowledge that play is the basis for learning and that the children are consistently solving the mysteries of their universe to extend their understanding of the world, then we need to consider how often we put a screeching halt to their discoveries. Children are asked to clean up very often. Typically, children are asked to clean up before group meeting times, playground time, snacks, and meals. Sometimes, we throw an extra clean-up time into the day when we feel like the room is a mess. I cannot imagine having someone walk into my office throughout the day and ask me to put everything on the desk away. Done or not, put the papers in their folders. I would venture a guess that I am not the only person who has things that I leave out at home and at work that I intend to return to for more detailed inspection. At home, my mail ends up on my dining room table. I intend to go back to it. There are ads for stores where I often shop, and statements from the insurance company. Eventually, a pile forms and I realize I'd better sort what requires my attention and what is actually garbage. My intention was to go back and, eventually, out of necessity, I do. How often do we ask children to put things away when they are not yet done exploring? How much learning is lost?

The truth is that deeper learning doesn't take place in 10 minutes, 30 minutes of center time, or even in just one day. I would have loved having just one day of chemistry in high school during which I learned all I needed to know and could move on to something else. We cannot learn deeply and extend that learning in just one day. Chemistry took an entire year of exploration. College students study a topic for a semester. When you enroll in a one-day cooking class or even a professional development conference, you know that you will merely scratch the surface of knowledge. You may walk away with a few new ideas but, even as adults, diving into a topic takes a longer commitment. Yet when teaching young children we change themes quickly, introduce new concepts in rapid succession, and adhere to schedules that don't give the opportunity for long-term exploration of what captures a child's curiosity.

Schools have schedules that divide the day into segments. Activities in the classroom cease when it is playground or gym time, lunchtime, or any other time that requires coordination of services among multiple classes. While moving out of your space or shifting to institutional activities is unavoidable, you should plan to have activities that span more than a day.

We tend to concentrate those efforts on science-based activities. We plant seeds and wait for plants to grow. We bring caterpillars, fish, and other animals into our classrooms to observe over time. More often than not, crafts happen just in one segment of one day. Literacy activities tend to be given a moment in time during group time or at a table but don't span on the calendar. Even if we are concentrating on one letter and its sound for multiple days, the planned activities are segmented. They also aren't based on the children's curiosity as much as our agenda.

When I say to a room full of early childhood professionals, "Play is anything that the children find to be fun," or "Deeper learning does not happen in short segments of individual days," everyone nods in agreement. We can acknowledge truth in these statements but that is not enough. Our actions need to support respect and value for children's need to expand learning over time. Parents often tell me that when they ask about their children's day, the children say, "We played." I explain to parents that to the children that means, "I had fun." That "fun" can and does include kindergarten readiness skills included in literacy, pre-math, cognitive, gross motor, science, fine motor, and other learning activities. We stretch what the children think is fun by asking open-ended questions to extend their thinking while they play, rather than setting the rules and the limits of every activity.

Play doesn't only mean dress-up. Play is sensory, thought-provoking, and extended by us. We extend children's discoveries by asking and not telling. Children love to ask us why. We need to ask it, too. "Why did you put that block there?" "Why did you paint with purple today?" "Why is the ice cube cold?" We need to challenge their actions and demonstrate that there is sometimes more than one way to solve a problem by asking, "How can you do it another way?"

Play is the hard brain work a child needs to do and wants to do. The work of childhood can look like children building a castle from blocks or designing a new route with train tracks. That work can also look like children at a table writing, if that is what has captured their interest. It looks like children digging in the sand and watching the sand pour through a sifter. It is a group of children releasing the butterflies that they have watched since they were caterpillars. Play is how children unravel the mysteries of the world. Fun and engagement of the senses, interpreted as "play" by the children, is how they learn best and should be the focus of planning for teachers. Engage as many senses as possible and remember that learning can and should be filled with joy.

CHAPTER 4 QUICK NOTES

Tips for extending learning through play:

- Recognize that children consider enjoyable activities to be play—at your table and throughout the classroom.
- Refrain from telling students to "Go play." If it was fun, it was play! When it is time to leave your table, ask what else they want to do.
- Wait to be invited into their play. Resist the temptation to insert your ideas.
- Allow for long-term play activities. Deeper learning happens over time.
- Ask open-ended questions about their play.
- Engage multiple senses in all activities.

CONVERSATION POINTS WHEN COMMUNICATING WITH PARENTS

- Parents need constant reinforcement that their children are learning through play. Remind parents that we relate to learning by remembering our last learning experiences—but that was in high school or college. Remind them that when they were younger, they learned from exploring, playing, and engaging their senses.

- Periodically send articles home that explain what the children learned while they were playing, pretending, building, and exploring. Articles are readily available on the Internet—that's the great part of having so much technology!

- When you share pictures of the children at play, provide an explanation of the learning that took place during the activity.

- Teach parents to ask open-ended questions about their children's play and to assume nothing. Just because it looks like a certain form of play or scene to us, doesn't mean that is what the children are thinking.

- Explain that it is through observing play that we learn how children view the world.

CHAPTER **5**

Socialization Expectations: You Cannot Fail Playing

Parents tour preschools and usually cite several reasons for wanting to find the right place for their child. Often, they express a desire to have their children succeed in a social setting with their peers. Parents recognize that their children need to learn about social interaction before elementary school. They recognize the need to build social skills but don't often clearly define signs of success. Adults need to remember that learning social skills is a process that is influenced by both nature and nurture.

An authoritative medical dictionary defines socialization as "the process by which a human being beginning at infancy acquires the habits, beliefs, and accumulated knowledge of society through education and training for adult status" (*Merriam-Webster's Medical Dictionary*, n.d.). It is so much more than two children being developmentally ready to play together. It is training for a lifetime of interaction with other human beings. Socialization is finding our place in the world based upon our experiences and individual perceptions.

A child's first day at preschool is an interesting study in the difference between how adults view the world and the children's actual perceptions. Parents bring their children to a room full of strangers and say, "Have fun!" The children don't know their teachers. They don't know if these new adults will help them when they need something or if the grownups will be kind and caring. They don't know most, if any, of the other children. They are tossed into the unknown and told to go interact with a bunch of people they have never seen before. It must be terrifying.

At the end of the day, the children are asked, "Did you play with anyone?" Parents tell me consistently that they want to be sure that their children are playing with others. Until approximately age four to five years old, playing *with* others is an unrealistic expectation (Is Your Child Achieving Milestones In The Developmental Sequence?, n.d.). That form of play, with consistent interaction, is how adults measure social success. I am a parent and I understand how desperately we all want our children to be loved. It makes us happy to see our children accepted and embraced by their peers. Many of us experienced the pain of rejection at some point in our childhoods, and we don't want our children to feel that hurt. From the time when they are very young, we look for signs that our own children will not suffer, that they will make friends easily, and be loved. This desire—this fear of our children being hurt—sets up an unrealistic expectation.

Until sometime in approximately the pre-kindergarten year, children simply cannot negotiate play well enough to cooperatively play with others. Cooperative play is marked by the ability to build, create, and participate together as a group—to work as a team. Teamwork is a part of social development but is not the first step. Children who play near and around each other are developing their social abilities. They are not being emotionally hurt or trying to hurt the feelings of others. The truth is that children cannot fail playing. They play to figure out the world, and however they do that should be acceptable. Adults should not measure socialization success by our perception of and need for popularity. Adult hurts and baggage have no place in the measure of a child's social development.

We also are unfair when we measure social success by a child's verbal intelligence. A child who is less verbal may be better at other activities. Likewise, a very verbal child might struggle to negotiate social interactions successfully. Socialization is an acquired skill. It needs to be nurtured and taught just like all other academic subjects. It doesn't just happen because we have brought a group of children together. Socialization in the early childhood years doesn't look like adults want it to look. It doesn't happen as quickly as so many parents or teachers hope.

Throughout our lives, socialization is a dance between our innate tendencies and what we have learned about engaging with one another. Every classroom has children who stand back and watch while others seem to enter talking. If we want children to feel safe and to develop a positive sense of self, we need to accept them for who they are when they enter a room. We need to remember who we are when we are in similar situations.

Imagine you are invited to a wedding and you won't know the other people there. You felt glad to be invited with a plus one because knowing someone tends to give us comfort in new situations. On the day of the wedding, your plus one is sick and cannot attend. How do you feel walking into a room filled with strangers?

I often ask this question during professional development presentations. Every time I ask, someone says, "I'd go to the bar," and everyone laughs because they recognize the shared underlying anxiety. The young children in your school cannot go to the bar to calm their nerves. They are exposed in the unpredictable situation into which they have been thrust. Each of them has a different way of finding their comfort zone. Teachers and parents just need to let them lead the way. The adults need to give the children the space to find their individual comfortable place among the strangers. A child's version of "going to the bar" to calm down may be going to the sand table alone for a little while, or finding a toy or book on the shelf that reminds them of home. We need to just let the children do what they need to do. Watch the children to see what items or activities they gravitate toward when the social situation is overwhelming.

Some of the children will enter the room with an item from home because that gives them the most comfort. I have spent a career welcoming children who refuse to take off their coat, leave their bag in the cubby, or give their toy from home back to a departing parent. I have asked teachers why they work so hard to separate children from their comfort items, particularly the toys from home. Teachers tell me that they worry that the toy will be lost or broken. They worry that the child in the coat will be too warm. They don't want the other children to want their bags, too. At that moment, the child is lost and needs that item. That need for comfort should supersede our own fears. Once the child feels more comfortable, the bag, coat, and toys will more easily be handed over.

Think about how you keep your items with you when you are unsure. I was recently at an event with a coat check. I wasn't sure if I wanted to stay at the event. I was asked if I would like to check my coat and I replied, "Not yet, thank you." The children are merely saying the same. When I felt more comfortable and realized that the event was a worthwhile use of my time, I did return to the coat check and handed over my jacket. I did become warm, and carrying my jacket would have been annoying. I came to that conclusion on my own. The children will, too. I did, however, continue to keep my purse with my most precious belongings on my arm. I didn't put it by the table and walk away. In the setting, I logically knew that I could put it by my chair, but I wasn't ready. Why do we expect children to be immediately ready when we often are not?

Adults seem to be most comfortable with children who will dive right into social interaction. But we do a disservice to many of our more introverted students when we don't recognize and honor their personality styles. In order for teachers and parents to communicate both verbally and nonverbally that all natural tendencies are acceptable, we need to understand that introverts are happy people too. For years, I have watched teachers and others who interact with children try to get them to interact even when they aren't ready yet. In fact, it seems that we do not fully understand the definition of an introvert versus an extrovert. Introverted is not necessarily synonymous with shy and afraid.

I spend many hours per day with other people. I talk with parents and staff. I teach in classrooms, present on stages, and move among crowds as I conduct lectures and presentations. In spite of my proven ability to skillfully interact with other people, I define myself as an introvert. I prefer standing on a stage and speaking to a crowd far more than entering a room where I will have to make small talk for hours. I become tired from social interaction and need quiet time to re-energize. I become energized from time alone, when I can be creative. These traits do not make me an unhappy person. I am only unhappy when people try to force me out of my comfort zone. We force children out of their comfort zones far too often.

Introverted children become tired and overwhelmed by the demands of endless social interaction. We need to respect their need for time apart. When their parents tell us that they fall asleep in the car before leaving the parking lot on the way home, they are giving us an important clue about their children—we need to recognize how the day filled with other people wore the child out. They are signaling their need to recharge by separating themselves from the crowd and giving in to the urge to sleep.

Extroverts, on the other hand, are energized from social interaction. Extroverted children seem to have endless energy. They do not fall asleep in the car on the way home. These children are more likely to resist going home to nap, and want to go to play with more children even after a full day at preschool. Their parents come to pick them up, and they are jumping up and down and are unwilling to leave the social situation in your classroom.

Recent studies have shown that there is a difference in brain development and chemistry between introverts and extroverts. Redstone Promotional Communications summarized the findings in an article on circkles.com (CIRCKLES MOTIVITY: "An Introvert's Brain vs. an Extrovert's Brain," n.d.).

> *In 2005, researchers . . . suggested that the real difference between extroverts and introverts may be related to dopamine—a chemical in the brain responsible for our feeling of being rewarded or fulfilled. In a study they conducted, researchers used a brain scanner to examine responses from participants who were doing a gambling task. They found that when gambling brought positive results, the extroverts exhibited a stronger response in two regions of the brain: the amygdala and the nucleus accumbens, showing that they processed surprise and reward differently than introverts. If extroverts responded more strongly to gambling paying off, they probably would respond more strongly to adventures, social challenges, or taking risks.*
>
> *More recently, in 2012, Randy Buckner of Harvard University discovered that introverts tended to have larger, thicker gray matter in their prefrontal cortex—a region of the brain that is linked to abstract thought and decision-making—while extroverts had less gray matter.*

A young child enters a room and stands in the middle of an empty space alone. He is hesitant to walk over to the other children who are already interacting. Adults will ask the child, "Do you want to play with them?" That is a pressure-filled question. Some children will give the answer they think will please the adult. Some children will answer honestly. It is hard for us to tell what the child really wants, and so we have said the wrong thing. We need to support the child's natural instinct to wait a moment, assess the situation, and find his way in, or to find his own comfortable place outside the crowd.

A more supportive response to the child standing outside the action would be, "Welcome! When you are ready, let me know if you want to play with them or if you want your own toy to play with." It's a message that says that it is acceptable to either join the crowd or not. It is an unrealistic expectation that every child wants to interact in the same way by being part of the crowd all the time. After all, that isn't true for every adult. We enter rooms and hesitate. We sometimes hope to be left alone while we pull out our smartphones to check for email. The same is true of children. Sometimes they want to interact. Sometimes they do not. Often, they hope to be left alone while they take a piece of clay or reach into the sandbox, and acclimate themselves to their surroundings in their own way.

When setting up our classrooms, we need to remember the times when we seek a quiet place, a place away from the interaction, and provide that for our students. As I travel from school to school consulting, I can easily see how classrooms are encouraging environments for our extroverts. There are so many places for interaction. Centers for dramatic play, building, manipulatives, and art are set up for multiple students. There are carpeted areas for many children to sit together. Even the literacy centers, often cozy with cute little chairs and miniature sofas, are for togetherness. It makes sense. In a room of 15 children, everyone should have a chance to choose their place for play. But what about the child who needs to recharge, regroup, and take a quiet moment?

Near the end of the day, I was in a classroom watching children at play. One three-year-old girl looked particularly forlorn. Her hair was disheveled in that "I've had a full day" way and she was visibly seeking a quiet place for herself. She took a piece of clay from the table, several children followed her, and she walked away. She went to the book area, opened a book, and another child sat down next to her. Again, she walked away. She wasn't making a fuss as she went from place to place, so no one perceived that she was in any kind of distress. I watched as she continually sought but failed to find a place where she could be alone. At her age, she doesn't have the capacity to say to a teacher, "Excuse me, but I'm trying to find a spot to be by myself." It was definitively what she was trying to do as she continued to try different spaces in the room and leave them when someone else walked over.

It reminded me of a celebration I had attended the weekend before this observation. There were about 100 people in a ballroom eating, dancing, and celebrating. The music was loud, and people had to shout to be heard. I knew most of the people there and was busy catching up with everyone and their news. At some point, I remember wanting a quiet moment. I went to the restroom but ended up engaging in conversation with people I hadn't seen in a while. I went to the lobby and was approached by several acquaintances. Eventually, I stepped outside. I breathed in the fresh but cold air, took a few moments to myself, and felt able to go back in to the interaction and the noise.

Our students cannot simply step outside. They are always with some-one—either their peers or with a teacher. In our classrooms, we need to consider their needs as much as we consider the need to ensure interaction. Somewhere in your classroom, set up a cozy space for one child. That can be the "quiet place." Teach the children that when they need quiet, they can go to the quiet place and, when a classmate is there, we will let him or her have some quiet time alone. Teach the children that alone time is not only acceptable but that it is good to enjoy your own company.

When more than one student needs a quiet place, move a chair or another comfortable seating object to a quiet spot for them. This is not a place that should ever be used to address inappropriate behavior. It is not a place for adult-imposed isolation for any reason. This is a place where children can self-select to be left to take a moment, and then reconnect with their peers when they are ready. It is a place where children learn a little bit about coping with socialization demands and their own needs.

We cannot change the nature of a child but we can nurture their desire to be socially successful. Being socially successful can mean different things to different children. One young child might express a desire to play with another group of children, and we can help facilitate that interaction. Another child might have had a successful day because she separated from her mother better than the day before, and we can applaud that bravery. Just as children develop individual literacy skills at their own rates, they develop social skills individually and only when they are ready. It is our job to send the message that they are fine being whoever they are and wherever they are on the developmental spectrum of social interaction.

Mildred Parten was a sociologist who studied the stages of play among young children. She classified different types of play in 1932, and her classifications are still used to define how children interact with each other and their environment. Parten listed six categories of social play: unoccupied, solitary, onlooker, parallel, associative, and cooperative (Parten, 1932). Each of these categories of play is considered normal for typically developing children. We can easily see examples of each type of play and the associated socialization in preschool classrooms:

- Unoccupied—The child is observing but not participating in play activities. The child stands back and seems to us to be unengaged or unsure of how to join with the others. It is true that some of the children are trying to figure out how to get into the crowd, but not all. As they are taking a moment to observe, so should we. We need to wait to see if they need us and not assume that they are unhappy watching. It is common for all of us to need a break from trying to navigate socialization and therefore just watch for a while.

- Solitary—The child is playing alone and is unaware of what other activities are occurring in the room. This is the child who is still playing and doesn't realize that everyone else is getting ready to go to the playground. Because the child is playing with a toy, the adults tend to be more satisfied than if the child is merely watching and so they don't push for more interaction until another child walks over. Then, adults tend to say, "She wants to play with you," and they feel compelled to make that interaction happen. We should look for the physical clues of a child who just wants to play alone. Children will often turn their backs, gather their items in their arms, or otherwise express that they do not wish to be with anyone else. We act as if this is a seminal moment in the child's development—if we don't force interaction at this exact moment, all will be lost. I have watched attempts at forced play so often during my consulting work that I can't help but wonder when it became wrong for adults to say, "He doesn't want to play right now. Let's leave him alone for a while." Teach children to honor each other's feelings by showing them to respect their peer's wishes—sometimes that wish will be to be left alone.

- Onlooker—The child is watching others at play and may talk to them but doesn't participate in the activity. A group of children may be playing with the sand in the sensory table. This child has not reached into the sand but is talking to and about the children who are digging. Others may be painting, and the onlooker interacts with them but has not picked up a brush to participate. When we see the children talking without arguing, we tend to be happy with the interaction. We pay less attention to the participation level of each child when they are exhibiting social behaviors such as conversation. We should just let this scene play out without forcing paintbrushes into unwilling hands. Often, watching and interacting in quick, small ways is an introvert's path back into the classroom's social scene. Introverts will naturally look to take a break—to be an unoccupied or solitary member of the class—but then need to find socially acceptable ways back into the group once the time alone has re-energized them. When I observe adults, it is apparent that we can be equally uncomfortable with the child who is slowly setting a path back in to interaction and the child who barrels in. I've observed the same teacher in one moment say, "Here's a train to play with them. Everyone move over," when the child wasn't yet ready and, in the next moment, say, "They are playing, leave them alone," to the child who jumps in and grabs a train. We send such mixed messages and they are all too often based on our own base reactions to the personalities in our classroom. Let the onlooker lead the way at his or her own pace and willingness to join the crowd.

- Parallel—Children are playing near each other but not together. They might imitate each other but they are not working together. Two children, for example, may have a pile of building blocks. They are next to each other but building two distinct structures. They may look over and imitate the use of material, but that is the sum total of their interaction. This is a socialization milestone for all children—introverts and extroverts alike. The willingness to be near without the desire or social skills to work together is an important step in the learning process. Just as children need to be able to identify letters of the alphabet out of order before they can master reading or writing, children need to be able to play near each other and notice each other before they can master interacting during play.

- Associative—Children are playing separately but interacting. During this type of play, children may be borrowing pieces of toys from each other but they are still not working at one activity together. Often among young children, it would be more accurate to say that they are stealing toys from each other. When children play associatively, we may hear cries of "She took my green one!" or notice more physicality like grabbing and shoving. The children become frustrated with each other's interactions as they work to complete their individual goals. When children begin to argue over toys and grab from each other, it is actually a sign that they are moving along nicely on the socialization continuum. They have gone from not caring who is around them, to noticing others, to interaction with others. While we need to teach appropriate ways to use toys, at the same time, we need to recognize that this "He took my block!" stage is progress. In my experience, this is the stage when we begin to be able to more accurately identify the introverts and extroverts. Extroverts are energized by social interaction, so we can watch their energy level increase during these grabbing and borrowing attempts at play together. Introverts, who become tired from interaction, will more likely and naturally seek breaks from the others. Both introverts and extroverts can become frustrated with the behavior of their classmates. Both may get upset, grab, throw, and cry. We need to remember that those reactions are about communication and not necessarily about the social characteristics of the child.

- Cooperative—The children are working together. They each have a role to play in the activity. They may be building one structure together or playing an organized game like duck, duck, goose. I notice this type of play most in pre-kindergarten classes and older. Walk into a room full of two-year-olds and there will be as many activities going on as there are children. Walk into a room with four- and five-year-olds and you will see one structure that they built together as a team.

I have seen children who are more introverted and children who are more extroverted go in and out of all these types of play. Sometimes, extroverted children are intrigued by an activity and can be found playing alone, while an introverted student helps with the tower several classmates are building together.

Introverts aren't alone when it comes to triggering adult concerns. There are times when extroverts draw adult attention by participating in an unexpected type of play. It isn't uncommon for teachers to worry about an extrovert who is suddenly choosing to play alone. Often, we take that as a sign that they aren't feeling well. Sometimes, in fact, children do step out of the fray when they are not well, but that isn't always true. More than once, I have seen teachers check children multiple times for fever when they weren't as gregarious as usual. Just like the introvert being pulled out of a comfort zone, the extrovert who is fussed over for choosing to play alone gets a message that their socialization isn't acceptable. Remember that all of us play in all these ways at different times.

As adults, we still consistently go in and out of these phases of social interaction. Sometimes, we watch others interact, but don't jump in, and we don't talk to those who do. Recently, I watched a group of adults play a game on the boardwalk at the beach. I did not talk to them. I did not play. I just watched and walked away. Other times, we talk to the participants but don't join them in their card game or board game. There are days when I parallel play. My son may be playing a game on his phone app that I am also playing, but not with him. One of our favorite activities is family game night, when we all play cooperatively together. When we choose to watch, we are not suffering. When we choose to play together, we haven't won some sort of socialization competition.

Throughout our lives and each day, our level of social interaction varies. It does the same for the children in our classrooms. If it is true that our reaction to other people speaks more about ourselves than about others, we need to consider whether our reactions to the range of socialization in our classrooms are more about us than the students. Our urge to get everyone interacting may say more about our own needs than the needs of the children. Our role is to teach, and our responsibility is to teach self-acceptance. When we push children into an activity where they aren't comfortable or try to fit children into a prescribed notion of what is best for their social interaction, then we demonstrate that they are not accepted if their tendencies are not to jump right in. That disparity between who they are and who we wish them to be sets up a learning environment that includes self-doubt.

Yet, it is our charge to teach socialization. We are creating citizens. We need to be clear about what that means. It does not mean that everyone interacts together all the time in the same way. It means that children learn about society. They learn the appropriate behavior for the society in which they live. They learn the different ways that people interact. They learn manners and etiquette and the roles of leader, follower, authority, and subordinate. They learn to function in multiple roles and in different situations. They do not need to be shoved out of their own comfort zones. They cannot fail playing. They need to find where they are most comfortable in their society. They need to be accepted and to accept each other. A world filled with leaders would not work. We need followers, bosses, workers, doers, and thinkers. A world filled with just introverts or just extroverts would be out of balance. We expect that different adults will play different roles in our society. The same should be expected of the children in our classrooms.

CHAPTER 5 QUICK NOTES

Maintain an atmosphere of acceptance of all levels of socialization.

- Set up a "quiet place" that children can self-select to recharge when tired by social interaction.
- There should be quiet places that accommodate one child only.
- Recognize that associative play—when children may argue over toys—is actually socialization progress.
- Do not force children out of their comfort zones.
- Refrain from imposing our fears about popularity.

- Teach children to respect each other's need for alone time by resisting the urge to force them to play together.

CONVERSATION POINTS WHEN COMMUNICATING WITH PARENTS

- Assure parents that children in the early childhood years rarely actually play together cooperatively. The ability to truly play with others develops as they approach the elementary school years. Today's parallel or solitary player can still be tomorrow's popular classmate!

- Assure parents that introverted kids are happy, too! We don't need to pull everyone out of their comfort zones. Remind parents how much they don't enjoy being put in social situations that don't feel comfortable.

- Teach parents that we need to respect who our children are today in order for them to gain the confidence to expand their socialization.

CHAPTER **6**

Behavioral Expectations: Creating Citizens Through Appropriate Expectations of Behavior

When I ask preschool teachers to name their biggest challenge, they say that it is behavior. The most requested topic for my presentations is about instituting a positive approach to discipline. Post-presentation surveys often list "challenging behaviors" as the topic that teachers would like to attend in the future. Teachers struggle most to address the children's behavior. They acknowledge that they feel like they could learn more, do more, and be more successful at teaching their young students to make good behavioral decisions. In order to address the variety of behaviors that challenge us, we must remember that appropriate behavior needs to be taught and learned, just like so many other life skills. The children's behavior is their means of communication, and we need to be objectively observing their behavior as we attempt to decipher their messages.

Preschool classrooms need to provide an environment that encourages academic, social, and behavioral exploration. Exploration requires some choice. As I travel from classroom to classroom in my career, I still see two very different styles of environment—teacher-led and student-led.

More than once, I have walked into classrooms to find that the teacher has selected everything—the art materials for the day, the book that will be read, the toys that are available for play. The teacher has also assigned play groups by instructing students which center they can go to or where to sit at which table. I always ask what factors played into these decisions because I am interested to know the strategy. Inevitably, the teacher has selected toys and materials that do not cause children to argue or grab and has set up the groups of children to ensure that there won't be conflict. If children don't experience conflict, how do they learn to negotiate? If our primary goal is to ensure the most comfortable day for everyone, including ourselves, we impede our students' learning. They need to make choices to learn differences, coping, and decision-making skills. The same is true for behavioral skills.

Socialization, behavior, and academics are inextricably intertwined as the components of a well-rounded early childhood experience. Individual behavior and awareness of one's behavioral options is as dependent upon the development of critical thinking skills as literacy, science, and other topics that are more traditionally identified as part of an early childhood curriculum. Just as adults don't become emotionally invested in the lines children trace or the shapes that they cut, we need to separate our emotions from the lessons the children need to learn about their own behavioral choices. Teachers need to be clear about their boundaries, their goals, and the steps they will take to teach young children about making appropriate behavioral decisions.

First and foremost, teachers need to be realistic in our expectations of behavior. We need to understand what children in the early childhood years can and cannot do without our assistance. We need to ensure that our expectations of these very young people are not more than we expect of ourselves. I was recently lecturing, and there were approximately 15 adults in a small room. Despite the fact that there was nowhere to be unseen, two of the attendees kept whispering to each other. It seemed that they were relating what I was saying to students they have taught, but they weren't willing to share with everyone. It was a whisper that reminded me of my grandfather's whisper when he was elderly and his hearing was failing. It was breathy but not quiet. The other attendees were clearly annoyed and kept turning toward them. I did that "stop talking until they get the hint" teacher strategy that we learn from generations of teachers who had perfected silence as a message. It didn't matter. They kept doing it. I wondered if they also go into their classrooms and admonish young children for talking to each other during their circle time. Think about the number of times you have been at a public event but couldn't resist whispering to someone.

I have stood in rooms large and small observing the entry of adults. Every time, without exception, the room fills from the back. Perhaps one or two people walk to the front and take a seat, but they are exceptions. It doesn't matter the venue, the type of event, or the characteristics of the typical attendee: rooms fill from the back row forward. Yet, we are forever trying to pull children closer to the action even when we like to hang back ourselves.

I went to a concert recently. An announcement was made that cell phones should be put away and pictures were prohibited. I turned to my friend and said, "Ugh. We can't take pictures?" She laughed and said, "You know everyone will." She was right. No one followed the stated rules. Cell phones were at the ready to take pictures, answer texts, and post on social media. Yet we bemoan the young children and their parents' inability to put down the electronics.

Just as the rule about no cell phones at the concert was not realistic, too many of our rules for our young students aren't either. Typical preschool classrooms have rules posted on a wall. Teachers write rules about being kind, taking turns, and using words. Decorative rule posters with pictures of our expectations adorn each classroom. Because these written rules can be seen by anyone, including licensing inspectors, school directors, and parents, we tend to be very careful in their focus and wording; however, typical preschool classrooms also have sets of unwritten rules. These are the rules that we repeat orally or enforce as events happen.

Often, these rules have much less to do with realistic expectations for behavior than with our own adult need for order and control. "Do not mix the Play-Doh" is one such rule. The students actually can mix the Play-Doh and learn a great deal from doing so. They learn about mixing and melding two different objects. Sometimes, the two colors make a marble-ized pattern. Sometimes, they meld to make a different color. Mixing the colors does not change the usability of the substance. When put back in the container with a lid properly in place, it will last just as long as if the colors were kept separately. Exposure to air ruins Play-Doh, not mixing colors. "Do not mix the Play-Doh" is a rule that is about our own OCD tendencies and our own need for order and control.

"Do not peel or break the crayons" is another rule about adult comfort rather than what is good for the children. Let the children peel and break the crayons. Peeling the wrapper makes the crayon easier to hold. The wrapper is on the crayon to remind the adults of the brand, so if the crayon was useful we will buy that brand again. Breaking crayons does not render them useless. In fact, they become tools for fine motor development. Smaller writing tools, such as broken crayons, force children to use their fingers to grasp, thus developing the muscles for a pincer grip. Full-size crayons are too easy to fist. Let go of your need for pristine crayons and encourage the children to break them. It's great hand exercise.

The rule "You cannot climb up the slide" is both detrimental to gross motor development and untrue. Children can, in fact, climb up a slide successfully. We need to spot them. Teachers need to be right there with their hands at the ready to support them. When children climb up a slide, they develop the muscles in their legs, arms, backs, and abdomens. It is good for coordination, as they are using oppositional motions of their hands and feet. They miss so many large motor muscle development opportunities when the rule is "you cannot climb up the slide." This rule is about an adult fear of children falling. They could fall from anywhere. They can be climbing up the steps of the slide and fall backward, but we don't tell them not to do that. We grew up with "you cannot climb up the slide" so it has stuck. The rule actually should be "one way on the slide." If children are climbing up, you cannot come down, and vice-versa.

Far too often, our unwritten rules for youth aren't even physically possible. Teachers see it as a mission to teach children to accept situations in which they must wait. They are asked to wait patiently all day long. They wait for classmates to join the line before leaving the room. They wait at a table for snack to be served. They wait for group time to begin because not everyone has gotten to the carpet. They wait for their teachers who need to corral everyone and then get the belongings that need to go with them to leave the room.

The ability to control impulses, to sit still, to wait, and to make decisions is governed by the frontal cortex of the brain. According to the National Institutes of Health, the frontal cortex matures at approximately age 25, not at age 5 (*NIH News in Health*, September 2005). Even when the frontal cortex is mature, we have a problem with waiting. When you are in the supermarket with a cart full of groceries, you look for the shortest line. When you sit in traffic, you get frustrated and annoyed. When you go to amusement parks, you sign up for any pass or ticket they offer that will help you to avoid the long line. You and I cannot wait either, and our brains are more fully developed! The notion that early childhood students will learn to wait is completely unrealistic. Some people in the supermarket are calm in line. Some children will be calm in the line in your classroom. Others will not. We need to have something to entertain them. Sing, dance, tell a funny story. They cannot simply wait for you.

While we are considering the difficulties that children face when having to wait in line, we need to think about the line itself. We ask two-, three- and four-year-olds to do the funniest thing—we ask them to line up and walk in a straight line. The line matters to us very much. We operate with the notion that the line keeps everyone safe. The students can, in fact, make it to the end of the hallway in a group. They can learn to move over when someone is coming the other way. Because adults have to stand in line wherever we go, we have made this a requirement for children of all ages. It is a convention of our society, and I cannot imagine sending a pre-kindergarten student to elementary school without knowing about standing in line. The preschool students don't, of course, care about my line. If they cared, we wouldn't spend so much time saying "You aren't in a line," or "Everyone pick a square on the floor to stand in." They do care about who the line leader is and who the caboose is because everyone in the middle is fairly anonymous. They like the attention that comes with being the line leader or caboose, but they really agree to stand in something resembling a line because it's the only way to get where they are going. I have seen teachers get very upset when the line falls apart on the way to the playground. Standing in line is not the most important behavior most teachers need to teach in a day. Expose the children to it, and let it go when the line isn't perfect. If we have to pick and choose what behavior will get most of our attention, standing in the perfect line should be very low on the list.

Rules of behavior need to be those that facilitate positive socialization. Establishing reasonable boundaries teaches that the world has rules and that those rules keep order. Children need to be taught to respect people, property, and the importance of health and safety (Harms, Clifford, Cryer, Harms 2014). Everything else is extraneous.

When your rules are precise and address only those three categories, children learn to distinguish between a rule and a preference. "Do not mix the Play-Doh" is a preference. The Play-Doh is still usable without repair, so by mixing the colors the children have not destroyed property. You can tell the children that you prefer the Play-Doh kept a certain way but, when that doesn't happen there shouldn't be consequences. Ripping a page out of a published book, however, is destruction of property, and falls outside the boundary that you set regarding respect for property. When a page is ripped out of a book, the book does not return to its original state. You may be able to tape it, but the book is forever changed to a diminished state. Teachers should not offer to "fix" the book with tape or staples. You cannot restore it to its original condition. You should explain to students that taping the book or putting staples in by hand actually does not "fix" it. It does not undo the damage. Therefore, "Do not rip books" is a reasonable rule to teach young students.

When students cross our reasonable boundaries—when they are not being respectful of people, property, and the importance of health and safety issues—we are given opportunities to teach. Our job as teachers is to instruct, and that includes instructing about behavior. It is not our job to punish children. Punishment is an attempt to eradicate a behavior rather than teach an appropriate response to a challenging situation.

Educators need to see challenging behavior as a moment in real time that they can use to educate everyone. Young children need to learn how to cope with frustration, think about their reactions, and value order over chaos. They need to develop an understanding that their decisions impact other people, and that the world responds when they behave beyond the limits. Just like when we teach children to write letters and numbers, lessons about behavior take time and repetition. The letter A is written the same way every time we try to write it. Behavior that is inappropriate must elicit the same response every time it occurs. That response must make sense and connect to the inappropriate action for it to make sense to the children and teach a valuable lesson. Adults must be predictable, because children who cannot separate fantasy from reality and have not yet developed enough executive functioning to accurately determine cause and effect need to see that every time they cross a particular boundary, the world will react the same way. It is, in fact, somewhat surprising to young children when adults react the same way over and over. Their experience must seem frenetic to them—one moment the water is cold and the next it is hot, today it is sunny and without explanation it begins to rain, one day their parents are happy and laughing, but the next people seem inexplicably sad and upset. The children don't understand the reasons for these changes and so they must seem so random.

The more consistent your reactions, the more you teach about the fact that there are consistencies in the world. Every time someone shoplifts, society reacts in the same way—there are definitive consequences. Every time a child hits, kicks, or reacts in a way that is not respectful, or risks health and safety, we need to react the same way. It is far more than an attempt to stop a behavior. It is a lesson about reactions and consequences from our own decision making.

Two children are playing with blocks. One child wants a block that his classmate is using, so he reaches over and grabs it. This causes a ruckus and, filled with frustration, they start to react physically. One child hits the other. This behavior breaks the rules about respect for people. The consequences for the behavior, however, shouldn't be punishment. Adult actions need to model the kindness we are trying to teach. If we do not want the students to yell at each other, intimidate each other, or speak to each other with disdain, we cannot model that behavior. The response of teachers needs to be guided by two questions: 1) What is a logical consequence of this behavior?; and 2) What behavior do I want to teach in place of this behavior?

When we don't instruct the children about a new and more appropriate behavior, we teach them nothing, and we cannot eradicate behaviors. We must replace them. Simply saying, "You are not allowed to hit!" does not teach the student what to do with the frustration. A logical consequence of unkind behavior in the block area is that the children need to leave the block area for a short time. When a child grabs, we need to teach her to ask for the desired object. When a child hits, we need to teach him to use words to say what he wants or to go to the teacher for help.

In our quest to teach independence, we tend to forget that teaching children to ask for help is a valuable lesson. Someday, the child might need help with a bully or with learning academics or with emotional issues. Learning that asking for help is preferable to suffering, even in typical preschool play, is a life lesson that they can carry with them for years to come. Saying, "Can I please have help?" can take more courage than continuing on a difficult path. In our classrooms, we should teach that asking for help is brave and honored. We need to respond to the request with kindness, reassurance, and tools for the children to draw upon should the situation occur again in the future.

The tools that we give to children need to relate to the particular situation that arose and society's rules. We need to avoid falling into a trap of using easy, quick, yet meaningless phrases to end unpleasant situations. Using the words "I'm sorry" when another person has been harmed is a societal custom that, when you think about it, makes little sense at best. Even as an adult when my feelings have been hurt, the words "I'm sorry" do not make that hurt disappear. When you are hurt by someone and they say, "I'm sorry," you are likely still hesitant about their future behavior. It is true that using the words "I'm sorry" is a convention of our society that indicates good manners, and therefore should be taught. Those two words cannot, however, be viewed as a teaching tool or a solution to a problem.

Consider the behavior of children who can say the words, "I'm sorry." What do they think those words mean? Because we force children to say, "I'm sorry," and then tell them to go back to playing or do whatever they were doing before, some children think those two words erase the deed. Some children will say, "I'm sorry" before performing the action that they know may be deemed unacceptable. They say, "I'm sorry" and then knock over your water. They also commit an offense that they know from past experience will attract negative attention and they say, "I'm sorry" quickly, as if that means they didn't just hit or kick their playmate. The words "I'm sorry" do not teach behavior. They do not state what was unacceptable. They do not summarize an important lesson, and they do not make the offense better. Teachers need to take the time to teach the lesson. We can only do that by having children say more than "I'm sorry." All too often, we use "I'm sorry" to end an episode so we can move on with our daily schedule. We state a perfunctory, "Say you're sorry" when there is conflict and we need to get to the playground. We may need to end the drama or chaos, but we need to take to the time to instruct about rather than attempt to erase the behavior. We need to have them say, "I'm sorry. I will not kick you again," or "I'm sorry. I will not grab from you again." Will they kick and grab again? Yes, probably. Eventually, one day, the child will realize that every time she kicks, the playing stops and she has to have this conversation. One bright shining day, she will realize that kicking again isn't worth it, or she will have gained the tools to use words instead of actions to express frustration. We don't know what day that will be, so every time she kicks, the same method of teaching needs to take place.

Until the children develop a more global view of the world and can see events from multiple perspectives, we need to be that lens for them. In the adult world that they will enter someday, people who don't meet their responsibilities experience consequences. The consequences are fairly consistent. If an adult fails to do his job well, he risks being fired from his job. If an adult breaks a law, she will experience legal penalties. Children need to learn that the world reacts to their actions and that those reactions will be the same every time. Fail to meet work responsibilities multiple times, and risk losing multiple jobs. Break the law more than once, and there will be legal consequences each time. Hit with a wooden block, and the consequence will be the same every time. Push a classmate, and the reaction of the world will be the same today, tomorrow, and the day after. The consequences need to be related to the inappropriate action, be enacted calmly as a matter of course, and be the same every time.

It isn't usually difficult for adults to figure out that a child who is behaving dangerously to others in the building area needs to be out of the building area for a short time. It is difficult, however, to separate ourselves and realize that the children aren't testing us. They don't get up in the morning at age two, three, or four years old thinking, "I'm going to get her today. I'm going to do everything to make her miserable." They are not testing our coping skills. They are testing their own power in the world. It is easier to remain calm and logical when we remove our own egocentric viewpoint from the situation and know that it isn't at all about us. We are here to teach and to guide. It is our responsibility to stay out of the power struggle. Getting into the dramatics of the situation teaches children that it is very grown-up to become emotional when times are tough. It is actually our charge to teach children to reflect, think, decide, and respond appropriately. Emphasizing the development and use of critical thinking skills and modeling those skills is our duty when we are teaching a lesson about appropriate behavior, not only when teaching a science, literacy, or other academic activity. Children will do what we do, not what we say. We can tell them to calm down, but if we aren't able to be calm they do not learn when to pay more attention to logic than emotion.

Teachers need to recognize the early childhood power struggle as children trying to find their power over their own lives and not as a personal challenge to the adults around them. All of us tend to personalize the behavior of others. We think everything that happens is because of or about us. The young person's power struggle is not, however, about us at all. Children are looking for opportunities to make their own decisions and own their own lives. Older methodologies taught that children need to be told what to do, what to play with, and how to accomplish every task.

When I began my career in early childhood education, it was very common for teachers to select those toys for their students. That was the norm and the expectation of the adult. Teachers would, and were expected to, pick the two or three toys of the day, put them on a table, and those toys were the permitted playthings. There might be other toys visible, but the children were taught and quickly understood that they could only use what the teachers placed in certain areas. I am grateful to still be an early childhood educator in a more enlightened time. We know the importance of student-led investigation. Children need those opportunities to make their own choices. The children who are most noncompliant, who refuse to do what is requested of them, often behave that way because they need to feel that they have some power. They need to be given more choices and not fewer, as often as possible. Teachers should consistently ask themselves when they could be giving more choices to the children in their classes. Even when their behavioral consequences include being asked to walk away from their chosen play areas, children need to regain equilibrium by ending the incident with a choice.

Consider how you feel when you cannot undo an unhappy situation and then you feel powerless. Imagine that you have gone to the dentist. The dentist tells you, "You have seven cavities and you must come on Tuesday to have them filled." You would be beside yourself. You cannot go back in time to try to undo the cavities, and now you have no choice about when to have your teeth filled. When you learn you have cavities and are allowed to schedule an appointment at what seems to be your own convenience, you are given a small amount of power back. You find comfort in fitting the next appointment into your schedule when you see fit. Think about your encounters at the dentist, doctor, or similar settings. Your appointment time isn't only according to your schedule. In fact, you are scheduling when the doctor or dentist can fit you in their calendar, and there are times when you have to rearrange prior commitments. The doctor or dentist is not rescheduling other patients to fit you in the calendar. It feels like you are choosing, but actually you will never see a doctor or dentist at a time that their calendar doesn't permit. You simply partake in the process of selecting time, and you do not feel forced or backed into a corner. It makes for a better experience than if they had been entirely honest and said, "Here's when you can come and that's that."

Compare this to the child in your classroom who hits a classmate with a block. The child cannot go back in time and undo the frustration or the action of hitting. The teacher might say, "You cannot play with blocks right now." It is important to give the child a modicum of emotional equilibrium by restoring a small amount of power. Give the child a choice of what he can do next. Ask him to choose between two other activities, perhaps puzzles or painting, before he will be permitted to go back to blocks. The choice between two new activities will help the student to feel less like the walls are closing in on him. When walls are closing in on us, we have to push them back. It is instinctual. The same is true when behavioral walls are boxing us in. The children won't need to push back as hard if they feel like they are not being walled in.

A boy in the class has been throwing sand from the sand table at the other children. The teacher brings the child to a chair near her, asks him to take a breath, and talks about how throwing sand can hurt the other children. The teacher knows that the logical consequence is that, for a short time, the child cannot play in the sand. Instead of telling the boy that he must color now, the teacher recognizes that she needs to help the child feel a little power again by giving a choice. She tells the young boy, "You cannot go to the sand right now. You can do a puzzle or color. Which one?" and the boy will undoubtedly say that he wants to go back to the sand. The teacher should repeat calmly and with a smile, "Puzzles or color. Which would you like to do?" The teacher may have to repeat the choices a few times, but the student will eventually choose, if for no other reason than to be able to leave his current seat—but he will choose, and he should choose, the next activity. Give him a little power back with two choices. Help him to refocus and see that he is not entirely powerless.

Behavioral decision making is just one more lesson on a list of lessons for the day. It is one more opportunity for adults to teach and model learned skills. We need to model appropriate behavior during every interaction we have with both the students and adults in our schools. The students are always watching, and they take lessons from what we do, including what we do with other adults. We tell children to use words rather than grab toys from each other. Then, when interacting with adults, we forget and we grab objects all the time. A parent walks into the classroom to tell the teacher of a different emergency phone number for the day. The teacher needs a pen but the assistant is using it to take attendance. The teacher walks over to the assistant who is holding the pen but not writing. She takes the pen out of her hand. The students observe this behavior and see that adults take things from each other's hands. It must be a very grown-up thing to do.

Likewise, we tell children that they shouldn't hit or push each other. That is not what their hands are used to do. In order to teach appropriate personal space, you may have a "no touching" rule, and that is perfectly acceptable provided that the adults adhere to it, too. A "no touching" rule has to apply to literally everyone. When an adult walks into the classroom and teases the teacher, the rule has to apply, so the teacher cannot playfully shove the jokester in the arm. For many of us, our instinct is to reach out and touch other people for a variety of reasons—when joking around, when trying to get the person's attention, when offering support—but you cannot have a rule that you can't also abide by. If you are going to tap and playfully shove and hug, expect your students to do the same.

The rules need to realistically and consistently apply to everyone. Determining the boundaries in your classroom takes a great deal of intentional thought. For every rule you impose and every request you make about behavior, you need to be sure you can enforce it every day and live it yourself. Every time a behavior occurs in your classroom that you wish to use as a teaching tool, you need to consider several questions about your response.

First, you need to carefully consider what behavior you wish to teach in place of the inappropriate behavior, and find a way to include the child in the lesson. Is the behavior you are about to teach possible for the young child, specific enough, and one that you will model? Can you facilitate a discussion that will help the child decide upon a more appropriate behavior?

When a student hits or pushes, you may want to teach that our hands are for our own bodies, but that doesn't give the child anything to do with the frustration that caused the action. Yes, our hands are for our own bodies, and for writing, building, drawing, and eating. The dilemma is that the child was upset and the instinct was to hit. Hitting was that child's way to communicate.

We may want to tell the child to use words but, realistically, if the child was able to come up with the correct words, that would have happened. Children may know vocabulary, but being able to use that vocabulary in times of upset is an entirely different skill. Often, we cannot find the words when we are upset, either. We tell people we were "speechless."

As adults, we have hopefully learned that even when we are speechless and upset, hitting people isn't the best policy. We need to help children to discover the other possible behaviors that can be used when they are frustrated with a classmate. When the drama has ended and everyone is calm, ask the child what else he or she might have done in that situation. Help them to be their own problem solvers. It is so much more powerful and more of a lasting lesson when the child can help to solve the problem.

Recently, I was standing in a classroom and watched a three-year-old girl push one of her classmates. She wanted to get by and he wouldn't move no matter how many times she said, "Move!"

Finally, she had no other tool left in her toolbox, and she pushed. I took her aside and said that I saw her push. I told her that pushing is not allowed because people can get hurt and it isn't kind. I asked her what else she could do. She thought for a moment and asked, "I could push myself?"

I realized that she remembered the teachers saying that her hands are for her own body. I smiled and said, "Try to push yourself. Can you?"

She put her hands to her chest and tried. She giggled and said, "No."

I said, "Well, what else can you try when people won't move out of your way?" She thought again. She said, "I could get you."

I said, "Yes. You can get me or another grownup. You can walk around the other way. There are other things you can do." I asked her what she will do next time.

She said, "I will go that way," as she pointed to another route. I told her to come with me to tell the boy who was pushed that she won't push again. She walked over to the boy and looked at me. I said, "Say 'I won't push you again. Next time, I will go that way'." And next time, we will remind her of her decision.

Keep in mind that young children need to learn that other people physically hurt like they do. They don't intrinsically know that everyone hurts the same way when their skin is hit, kicked, or bleeding. As part of the lesson, teachers need to teach that being hurt is a global experience. When children experience getting hurt, try to remember it so you can use the injury as a reference tool.

A three-year-old student returned from a family trip and told the staff a tale of getting hurt. He fell and cut his chin. It was traumatic. We knew it left an impression because he spoke so passionately about the incident. A few days later, the same student hit a classmate out of frustration. The teacher taught him not only that hitting isn't allowed but that hitting hurts skin, not unlike when his skin was hurt on the trip. He looked thoughtful when the teacher formed that analogy by saying, "Hitting him hurts his skin like when your chin got hurt." He obviously hadn't considered that other people's skin could hurt.

Because early learners are so egocentric, it is helpful to make the lesson about their own experiences. Another time, a student complained to her teacher about having fallen at home. She told the teacher that it hurt when she bumped her head. The teacher reminded her of that bump weeks later when she pushed a classmate, forcing her to bump into a toy cabinet. The hurt is the same. She also quietly took that in with a thoughtful expression on her face. Remember their egocentrism when trying to teach that a behavior needs to be replaced with another.

Additionally, teachers need to recognize when they are rewarding the inappropriate behavior. For every behavior there is a reward. If there is no reward, nothing we get from our behavior, we don't repeat it. When I ask rooms filled with teachers what reward most children want from their actions, they respond that children want attention. Positive or negative attention—it often doesn't matter. From the time children are babies, they look for our reactions. If an infant laughs and it draws our attention, they will continue to laugh. If an infant throws things and it draws our attention, they will continue to throw things. We need to ask ourselves how much time we are spending attending to acceptable and unacceptable behavior.

Ideally, we make a concerted effort to pay more attention to good behavior. Unfortunately, we are too often afraid to break some sort of magical spell when children are interacting nicely together. It happens in classrooms all the time. A group of children are working well together in the kitchen area. We are afraid to go too near them because we believe that the spell will be broken and our presence will remind them that they should be arguing. We tiptoe. We tell other adults who enter the space to tiptoe and ignore them because they are getting along so well. It is the exact opposite of what we should do.

We need to acknowledge the good behavior more than the challenging behavior. When the children who ordinarily bicker are playing nicely in the corner, we need to offer positive attention. Stop tiptoeing and shushing everyone who enters. Instead, go to the children and tell them, "I like the way you are playing together so kindly and nicely. You should be proud of yourselves." Then walk away. There is a difference between breaking the spell and noting the good. If you were breaking the spell, you would be stopping the playtime, but you are not. You are simply pointing out a happy situation and going back to what you were doing.

Use the situation to teach the children about pride and the feeling of being proud of themselves. Don't make their use of appropriate behavioral skills about you. Tell the children they should be proud of themselves, not that you are proud of them. They need to integrate the feeling of pride. They will see that you noticed them doing the right thing. They should be happy with themselves.

Far too often, we spend our days putting out fires. Without a strategy, we go from one dramatic event to another and teach very little. We lose sight of the knowledge that approaching challenging behavior in the classroom is about teaching and not about preventing children from crying. We forget that we should not be emotionally involved in the upset, but instead need to help the children develop reasoning skills.

Finally, we need to keep in mind that we can only try to change one behavior at a time. A student may be exhibiting several challenging behaviors. Teachers need to prioritize. What behavior needs to be changed to a new behavior first? What behaviors can wait? We often think of children who communicate their frustrations with inappropriate physical behavior when we consider the challenges in our classroom, but a system of priorities applies to all human behavior.

One year, a new student joined the class in the spring. The other students had learned so much about daily routines and appropriate group behaviors that the new student's lack of experience really showed. He didn't know what was expected while sitting at a table and eating lunch with peers. He didn't know how and where to throw garbage away. He didn't know how to zip his lunch box or where to put it when lunch was over. I was in the classroom one day when the teacher asked him to throw out his garbage, zip his lunchbox, and put it with the others. He ignored her request. It was too much. She was trying to teach too many new behaviors at one time. I asked her to pick one. I asked, "Which is most important to you—the garbage, zipping, or placing the lunchbox?" She chose throwing the garbage in the garbage can. I told her that this task has to be mastered before she could move onto zipping or lunchbox placement.

The same is true for the student who hits, kicks, and tries to run from the classroom. The teacher has to decide which need is most immediate—staying in the room without an attempt to escape, expressing frustration some other way than hitting, or learning not to kick when people stand in the way. While it is a harder choice when all the behavioral concerns impact health and safety, adults still must choose. One behavior at a time, one step at a time—that is how we learn all new skills.

At the end of every day, we need to reflect so we can better plan for teaching behavior tomorrow. During your journey home or during a few quiet moments before you leave work, ask yourself, "What went well today? What didn't go well? How can I react better next time?" At the end of every day, think about your role in their need to feel powerful. Did you give enough choices today? Do the children feel like they can make decisions even when one activity isn't available to them? Think about your job as a role model of kindness. When the moment was challenging, were you kind in your approach to behavior? Did you honor their emotions while helping them to find alternative solutions to their problems? We stop being emotional firefighters when we give situations thought and have an intention.

CHAPTER 6 QUICK NOTES

Guiding questions for teaching behavior:

- What is a logical consequence of this behavior?
- What behavior do I want to teach in place of this behavior?

Steps to Addressing Behavior that Is Contradictory to Respect for People, Respect for Property, or Health and Safety

Bring the child to you. Clearly state the action that is not allowed. The action should be your first word in the sentence. For example:

1. "Hitting is not allowed."
2. "Pushing is not allowed."
3. "Throwing the blocks is not allowed."

Teach empathy. Follow up your first sentence with the reason that the behavior is not allowed by relating it to the child who performed the action. To do this, it is best to remember times when the children have gotten hurt to teach that other people can hurt like that, too. For example:

- "Hitting is not allowed. Hitting hurts his skin just like when you fell on the playground yesterday."
- "Pushing is not allowed. Pushing can bang her head just like when you banged your head on the bookcase."
- "Throwing blocks is not allowed. The block can hurt his eye like when you fell on your stairs at home."

Ask the child to go to the victim and say they are sorry and state what they will not do again. For example:

- "I'm sorry. I will not hit you again."
- "I'm sorry. I will not push you again."
- "I'm sorry. I will not throw a block at you again."

Give the child a choice of two other activities. Calmly repeat the choice until the child chooses.

When the child wants to return to the original activity, remind the child of your expectation. For example:

- "Blocks are for building. You can go there and build."
- If the inappropriate behavior is repeated, repeat all the steps above.

Next is an example of the parts of your conversation with a child who needs to learn about a behavior. In this example, the child hit a classmate. This phrasing is the same regardless of the particular action.

PHRASING YOUR RESPONSE—SAY THE ACTION FIRST:

Example	*Do* calmly say	*Don't* say
The child hits a classmate.	Hitting is not allowed.	You aren't allowed to hit.
	Hitting is not kind.	You aren't being nice.
	Hitting hurts people.	You hurt her.

TEACHING EMPATHY:

Example	*Do* calmly say	*Don't* say
The child hits a classmate.	Hitting hurts her skin.	Look at her crying!!
	Her skin hurts like when you . . . (name one of the times the child who hit was hurt) fell on your knee last week.	She got hurt. Look at her arm!

MAKE THE APOLOGY MEANINGFUL.

Example	*Do* calmly request	*Don't* say
The child hits a classmate.	Tell your classmate, "I am sorry. I won't hit you again."	"Tell her you are sorry."
	If the child refuses to say the sentence or cannot, with the child right next to you, say, "He is going to be kind and keep his hands on his own body." State the expectations without apologizing for the child.	"He is sorry."

CONCLUDE THE BEHAVIOR LESSON WITH CHOICES.

Example	*Do* calmly say and repeat if necessary:	*Don't* say
The child hits a classmate.	"Now you can either to go . . . or . . .. Which one would you like to do? (i.e., puzzles or coloring)	"Now you can't go back over there. Pick something else to do."

CONVERSATION POINTS WHEN COMMUNICATING WITH PARENTS

- Assure parents that their children's behavior is about their children's power struggle. The children do not set an intention to battle their adults in the early childhood years. When we don't remain calm, we enter the battle of our own accord.

- Remind parents that they are role models of calm, coping, and respect, so even challenging behaviors need intentional, careful responses. To learn calmness, children need to see calm.

- Share as much information about how to calmly and rationally teach behavior as possible—making the action the subject of the sentence, explaining that other people can hurt, and so on—so parents are empowered with knowledge. Children need to know that we are all on the same page so we should all be approaching behavior similarly.

- Assure parents that we are all human and we all get frustrated. They can even model apologizing when their reaction to the children's behavior is emotionally charged and not instructive.

CHAPTER 7

Emotional Capacity: Sometimes Children Have a Bad Day, Too

Of all the unrealistic expectations of young children, the notion that every day should be replete with happiness may be the most impossible to achieve. We want our classrooms to be the happiest place every day. The problem with having the unspoken goal that our classrooms should always be happy is that our classrooms are filled with human beings. No human being is thrilled every day. Adults wake up in bad moods, and so do children. Adults may start the day just fine and our moods are changed by circumstances. The same is true for children. Unrelenting happiness is not realistic. Acting as if constant happiness is possible doesn't teach children what they need to learn to be functioning adults. It doesn't teach them to cope. Happy moments are great. They are not, however, the sum total of anyone's real life.

Happiness should be enjoyed but shouldn't be a goal. The children in our classrooms shouldn't feel that the day is better if everyone is happy. They shouldn't be burdened with the notion that their happiness influences the mood of the teachers. I can't help but wonder if people who are people pleasers and want everyone to be happy were in environments as children that valued happiness over all other emotions.

Happiness is merely one emotion in a continuum. Sadness, anger, anxiety, and frustration are just as acceptable. Our emotions come and go. They last for a while and another takes over. As teachers, we need to honor all the emotions that children feel and not value one more than the others. Constant happiness isn't achievable. It is a wish. It is not reality.

The goal for teaching emotional intelligence in our classrooms should be that all emotions are a normal part of being human. Emotions have names, and our bodies react to them. Feeling a variety of emotions is simply a part of the day for all of us. The lesson that we need to learn as we get older is that people can cope with whatever comes along. We need to teach children that they are also capable of doing so. We need to teach emotional strategies like we teach other skill strategies in the curriculum.

When we recognize that all emotions are part of the human condition, we are better able to honor all the emotions of our young students. The word "don't" needs to be removed from our reaction to children's emotions. "Don't be afraid." "Don't be angry." "Don't cry." Generations of parents told their sobbing children, "Stop crying or I will give you something to cry about." If the child is crying, to him or her there *is* something to cry about.

Parents in my generation roll their eyes at the memory of being told that we would be given something to cry about and, yet, many of us can catch ourselves saying, "Don't cry." It is equally invalidating. Crying is the normal bodily reaction to sadness. Likewise, telling a scared child not to be afraid sends the message that fear is an unacceptable emotion.

Emotions are never inappropriate or unacceptable. They are what the person is feeling. We are all entitled to feel whatever we feel. The lessons about emotional intelligence should be about what to do with those feelings in order to cope with their presence. The lessons are not about eliminating less comfortable emotional responses.

One of the most offensive things that we can say to children about their feelings is, "You are being silly," yet I hear adults say it all the time. I've heard frustrated parents say that at preschool when their children were angry or upset. I've heard people say, "You're being silly," in stores when children are upset at not being able to purchase a much wanted toy.

Imagine being in the midst of one of those days when everything seems to be going wrong. Perhaps you hit unexpected traffic in the morning and were late for work. Then, you realized your lunch was left at home on the kitchen counter. Your most challenging student challenged you even more today. You go home frustrated and annoyed and someone says to you, "You are being silly." How would that make you feel? While "Don't cry" and "Don't be scared" are invalidating, "You are being silly" is just offensive.

Psychology Today defines emotional intelligence as ". . . the ability to identify and manage your own emotions and the emotions of others." (Emotional Intelligence/*Psychology Today*, n.d.) Thus, our emotional intelligence as teachers includes the ability to identify and manage our own emotions, as well as being able to apply that knowledge to the lessons we teach our students about their emotions. We need to spend time becoming more in tune with our own feelings, accepting them, and considering how we cope, so we can pass the best of our emotional skills along to our students.

When I went to college, we took courses in educational psychology and child psychology to learn about the theories regarding how children think, learn, and express themselves. There was little, if any, self-examination. It creates a disconnect between teachers and students when we are focused on just them rather than on all of us. My emotions are as much of my wholeness as their emotions are of theirs. Our emotions are an integral part of our social interactions, our ability to absorb new information, and our capacity to form relationships. Our ability to recognize emotions, separate them from facts, and move forward by making good decisions is a learned skill. Our challenge is that, just like reading, writing, math, and science, we need to learn emotion skills before we can impart knowledge. Teachers cannot teach a student to write the letter "Aa" if they cannot write it. Teachers cannot teach subtraction if they cannot subtract. Teachers cannot teach students to recognize their feelings and cope if they cannot do the same. After years of working with children of all ages, but especially preschoolers, I realize that the colleges' courses about psychology should have also been about the adults and that a professional development requirement should include a little therapy as well.

Students watch what you do. They imitate your abilities and your shortcomings. If you teach them to write the letter Z from the bottom up instead of top down, they will do it. If you spoon water instead of pour it, they will spoon the water. If you show them that you can be upset but still think and make decisions, they will try that, too. You are the role model for emotional intelligence, so the work to be done starts with you.

Teachers have mantras—practice makes perfect, patience is a virtue. We say them to ourselves and to our students. We need to add to our list of mantras. We need to accept about ourselves, and then teach our young students:

- Emotions are normal.
- Our emotions are all acceptable.
- Emotions come and go.
- Emotions are not facts.
- We cannot always control our emotional instincts but we can control our reactions to them.

Self-examination is hard. Accepting our emotions is difficult if we come from a childhood filled with "Don't cry" or "Don't be afraid." Cry. Be afraid. Take a breath. Separate your emotions from facts. Make decisions after that. Teachers have an obligation to do the work that is required to separate ourselves from our own upbringings and look at the facts of emotions.

When children are feeling emotion, they get lost in it. Sadness overtakes them and they weep. Anyone who works with young children has had the experience of soothing a crying child who doesn't remember the source of the sadness. Sometimes, children cry and the reason for the tears becomes secondary to the presence of overwhelming emotion. Given a moment, they may recall that their toy was taken, but the immediate need has become the level of their own frustration and sadness.

On the other hand, sometimes children become fixated on the reason for their sadness. They wanted the green block. There is an identical green block but that won't do. They must have the one they desired. Their sadness quickly disappears when they are handed the toy that they desire. Happiness can also be all consuming, and children will sometimes literally jump with joy. The emotions sweep over them and they become involved in their expression with their whole beings.

When distraught, they plop themselves down and swing their fists. When thrilled, they jump up and down, clap, and twirl. The expression of emotions among early learners has not yet been tempered with self-consciousness, emotional awareness, and skills for coping. Therein lies our job. Our job is to show that you needn't feel shame when sad, angry, or scared. We are tasked with teaching the self-acceptance and coping skills that make emotions give way to thoughtful reactions.

First, practice emotional acceptance in your own life. That childhood message that you received when adults told you not to cry or not to be scared was not the right message. Accept the range of emotions as a part of being human. The question before you is not how quickly your feelings will go away, but what you can do to cope and to help yourself to find emotional equilibrium—a state of being where one emotion is not overwhelming. It is fine to be scared. Fear is your brain's way of protecting you. Fear is not fact. How many times have to been afraid of a confrontation that never happened? The fear existed to prepare you for the possibility of an unpleasant situation, but the situation never materialized. The fear was based on what you imagined might happen. It was a bit of adult pretend. When you feel worried or scared, the source of your feelings may or may not actually happen. Even if it does, you are strong, capable, and can figure out what to do next.

In early childhood, a common fear is being left to manage without your parents nearby. It is so common that it has been given its own name—separation anxiety. Young children are afraid of what will happen when their most trusted adults leave the room. The children have a real reason to be afraid. Anything might happen, and their protectors will not be there to save them. They truly believe anything can happen because they are unclear about the bounds of reality. If wolves can blow hard and knock down houses and superheroes can fly, then surely something can happen in the classroom that will be bad. "Do not be afraid" is the wrong message. The child is already afraid. You are too late and unrealistic. Our expectation actually should be that every child will be afraid. If a child is not fearful in a new situation, that is the unusual circumstance. The message to the frightened child should be "You can do this and I will help you." The student needs proof that this is a safe place filled with understanding people who will help when all seems lost.

When young children fall, they may cry from an injury or just from the surprise. Falling, especially unexpectedly, is a frightening situation. Last year, I was walking in a parking lot and didn't see the black ice beneath my feet. I took a step and the next thing I knew, I was down. My knee was cut open and bleeding. I was shocked. I had a renewed sympathy for young students who suddenly find themselves flat on the ground. "Don't cry" is as unrealistic a statement as a person can say in that situation. "That was scary. That hurt," validates the situation and the normal emotions. I would agree with any child that a sudden or painful fall warrants some tears.

I want every young learner in my classrooms to feel accepted and secure enough to look at me and cry, stomp, wave their arms in the air, and flail with emotion. Then, I want to help them label the emotion with a word. I want them to know it is acceptable to feel whatever you feel.

I want them to be able to make decisions even in the face of emotional upset and to be able to learn to choose a new path.

We cannot think clearly when we are upset and we need to slow the body's reaction to stress. When we are stressed, the functioning of the prefrontal cortex is impacted by the adrenaline and stress hormones that surge through our bodies. Our brain function is literally diminished in those emotional moments (Arnsten, 2009).

The ability to keep our bodies calm enough to think logically begins with one breath. One deep breath starts the pathway from emotion to logic. One, two, three deep breaths send a signal to our bodies that all is well, the adrenaline can stop pumping, and logical thinking can take over. When I am in a classroom and upset, I take deep breaths. Students may ask what I am doing. I teach them that I am taking deep breaths because I am sad or angry and need to think about what to do now. When they see a teacher do that, they will learn to do the same. The teacher has modeled the first step of coping.

When a student has been overtaken by emotion and we need to bring him to the present moment, we need to try to break the emotional cycle—the wall—that seems to stand between us. I have had many experiences during which I am calm and in the present moment, but the child is like a tornado of upset. Two three-year-olds were struggling over a favorite classroom toy. It was a beloved merry-go-round toy that someone had donated to the classroom—one of those old and irreplaceable toys that was often the subject of arguments simply because we only had one. On one particular day, the struggle was so intense and the child who wanted the toy was so frustrated that he started to flail his arms, scream, and have what I call an anger tantrum. In the midst of any tantrum, a child cannot really hear our requests. "Joey, calm down. Listen to me!" falls on deaf ears. I knew there was a way that I could try to bring him out of that cloud of anger. I needed to engage his senses.

As an adult, I learned mindfulness techniques that I wish I knew many years before. I'm fairly certain that I've spent most of my life thinking about the past, worrying about the future, and rarely existing in the present moment. Bringing ourselves out of past frustrations, futuristic worry, and overwhelming emotion is as simple as noticing the sights and sounds around us. As an adult, I am able to take a few deep breaths and engage my senses. I close my eyes and ask myself to:

- Feel the floor beneath my feet.
- Identify three sounds that I currently hear.
- Open my eyes and name the first three things I see.

It is amazing how that simple exercise can ground us. Teachers should practice this exercise and any others that they find helpful in this way, so they become more aware of the present moment themselves and can experience how beneficial simply noticing the present can be.

It is a bit more difficult to teach very young children to take those steps on their own, but they can be adapted. I was speaking with a group of parents about behavior when a social worker gave the best example I've heard of a quick way to engage the senses. She said that when someone she is working with is very upset, she asks that they put their hands on a cool countertop. Preschool classroom tables are great tools for this sort of immediate sensory engagement—they are often smooth and cool. Our classrooms are also full of sensory items that we can use. "Put your hands on the table" is so simple and can break the emotional spell. After she said that, I was in a classroom with a very frustrated child. I said, "Put your hands here" and put my hands on the table. I think the oddity of the request itself gave the child pause, and he did it. I could see him immediately calm down a bit. It caused a shift—a visible shift—in attention. When they are calmer, we can ask them to notice what they hear, see, and feel. When we do, we are guiding them in the steps of mindfulness and teaching them a coping skill that they can carry with them for their entire lives.

When our students can hear us, after we have helped them to find a way through the turbulence of strong emotions, we can help give thought and logic to their emotional situations. First, they need to be able to name their feelings. "What are you feeling?" is very different than the more common question, "What is wrong?" Identifying just the event ("He took my block.") does not create emotional intelligence. When we teach emotion words as we read books or have discussions with our students, we need to be mindful of the goal that they use their new emotion vocabulary to describe themselves. It isn't enough to just be able to identify a picture of a sad person. They need to be able to identify it in themselves.

"I am mad." "I am sad." The block has been taken and now I feel this. It is an early childhood accomplishment to be able to name your own emotions. It is an accomplishment for anyone to own our emotions without self-recrimination. When the emotion has been identified and owned, then the child can be helped to find a solution to the problem that caused the upset. A science experiment fails and we talk about what went wrong and what we could do differently. We guide students in trying different tactics to make the scientific situation work. The same should hold true for their emotions.

Managing emotions involves the same steps as any other puzzle. Children need to be guided through those steps:

1. What are you feeling?
2. Why are you feeling that?
3. What can you try?
4. What else can you try?
5. What was the result?

We can teach children to apply logic to emotion with open-ended questions just as we can teach children to apply logic to any other event with similar open-ended questions. They can become critical thinkers about the events in their own lives.

Preschoolers get so angry when someone takes their toy. They should be angry. Something that matters to them was just yanked from them. When I am using my laptop and someone walks over and grabs it, I don't like it either.

1. What are you feeling? Ultimately, I want a child to be able to say, "I am mad," or "I am sad," or however they, themselves, identify the feeling in their mind and body. At first, we need to give the vocabulary by saying, "I see you are mad." We should guide the child by adding, "Can you say 'I am mad'?" When we identify their emotions because they do not yet have the vocabulary, we need to be sure to be precise and identify the child's actual emotion, and not what we would feel. A situation that would make me angry might make someone else sad. We need to be in tune enough to the physical clues to be able to give them the correct vocabulary word. When we do, they will learn to answer the question appropriately.

2. Why are you feeling that? This is the first step in finding a solution to the emotional puzzle. This is the fact. This is the reality that could happen over and over and requires strategizing. "She took my green block." That's a fact and not a feeling. That is something that teacher and student can work with together. The feelings are what they are, but the facts can be considered without emotion.

3. What can you try? The classmate took the green block. The next time that happens, what can the student do? As with any intellectual lesson, it is best if the students can come up with strategies. It is faster when we tell them (use your words, tell her this or that) but it is a more valuable lesson if we give the learner time to think and come up with a suggestion or two. Of course, preschoolers may

have no clue what to suggest when something new and surprising happens. In that case, we should still be asking questions instead of making statements. "Can you say something to her next time?" and "What can you say?" stimulates their thought processes. I am reminded of that old adage about the importance of teaching a man to fish: "Give a man a fish and you feed him for a day; teach a man to fish and you feed him for a lifetime." Some lessons are timeless.

4. What else can you try? This question is so important when it comes to thinking about our emotions. Not every plan works. Not every strategy will work every time. A preschooler's emotional toolbox needs to be filled with possibilities. As adults, we spend time imagining different scenarios and outcomes when we have a problem. We imagine conversations going a variety of ways, and our possible responses. We cannot control the thoughts and reactions of others, but we can have a few strategies in mind to solve the problem. Preschoolers need to know that when they say, "I am using the green block," and their classmate grabs anyway, there is more than one strategy for solving that problem. The child can use words, try offering another block, or ask a teacher for help. Most situations have more than onc solution.

5. What was the result? This is the reflection question. When the block was taken, what happened? Preschoolers may say, "I cried," or "I can't build," or "She got the block." That means that we need a different action. Next time, if the same situation occurs, perhaps the preschooler will remember to say, "I'm using it." The result may be the same. Something else still needs to be done. We can reflect with the preschooler and remember that asking a teacher for help was another one of our solutions. We can encourage the preschooler to try another tool in the strategy tool box next time, to see what gives the desired result. It is the trial and error, and try again, that frames all of our lives.

Our role as the model of emotional intelligence is complex. We need to not only show that we can cope but demonstrate that we also experience a range of emotion. Just as we should not expect happiness all the time, we should demonstrate that we are not happy all the time, but we can still think and find ways to solve problems. My very grown-up problems should not be discussed with them, but my emotions certainly can be examples for them.

Over the course of a career, we experience the ebb and flow of life. That includes joyous occasions as well as losses. One year, my great-uncle died. He was the last of his generation in my family and the last link to my grandparents. He had led a full and long life. I was grateful that my own two children had that connection to a bygone era. He was one of those people who we thought would always be here. I was sad. I wanted my students to know that adults can be sad and manage it. Students don't need to know the details. They need to see the coping. In situations like that, I will mention in conversation at the craft table or the literacy table that I am sad today. Young children will react to our statements in ways that tell us about their experience with sadness. Some will not know what to do. Some may not react at all. Always there are young children who want to reach out to me, hug me, or otherwise pay special attention. If they ask, I tell them that something happened in my family (Imagine, children! I have a family!) and it made me feel sad. I let them see me consider my options. I tell them that maybe, if we sing a song, I will be less sad or if we can draw for a while, that might cheer me up. Even the children who did not know where to look or what to do when I said that I was sad will see that I am trying to find activities to help to me get on with my day. I would never take this to the level of making children my confidants. I use it as a lesson at their emotional and developmental level.

Other times, unexpectedly joyous events happen in our lives. I share happiness, too. Even happiness needs coping mechanisms. I can be happy about a personal event when serious matters need to be addressed in my workplace. I cannot let the happiness sweep me so far away that I cannot function in my everyday life. I can take moments to savor it, and then it's back to my responsibilities. The same is true for our students. Sometimes, I will mention in conversation that I'm so happy. Something thrilling has happened in my life. I ask the preschoolers what I should do. I love when they suggest that I shout, "Hurray!" like in the song "If You're Happy and You Know It." I also get a kick out of their suggestions to dance. Often, they don't know what to suggest because their happiness hasn't required any strategy. They just get to be happy. Teachers can and should tell them that we will shout "Hurray!" or dance for a moment, and then we are going back to the things we need to do. I tell students, "I'm going to do a happy dance and then I'm getting the glue for our project." I'm celebrating my joy and feeling good while attending to needed tasks.

They need to see adults coping with real-life ups and downs on a level that they can relate to, and they need to see us cope when their actions cause upset. Children are smart. They often know when their actions will upset the adults. I have seen very young children tell each other, "Don't tell her," because they know that whatever they have done will not be acceptable to the adults. As a teacher, my facial expressions and tone can change but only to ones that are authoritative and not any that may indicate that I cannot control myself. Teachers can frown, shake our heads, and furl our brows. Children need to know the nonverbal clues that indicate an unhappy emotion. Our students spend a great deal of time in front of screens looking at nonhuman characters—cartoons, puppets, and so on—that don't accurately model nonverbal communication clues. We have to help them to understand nonverbal clues from our interactions with them and their interactions with each other.

When I speak with them, my tone can become serious but not biting. Yelling is only necessary when someone is about to get hurt. It is an atten-tion getter in times of danger. It is not an appropriate reaction to emotion. Even when a teacher has to raise a voice to save someone from injury, it is appropriate afterward to say, "I am sorry that I yelled. I needed to save Joey from getting hurt. I will only yell if someone is getting hurt." I will yell in a medical emergency, not when your behavior triggers something in me that feels like anger.

Anger and frustration in young children are often expressed as a tantrum. A tantrum is a physical reaction to an emotional upset. It is an expression of distress that is loud and physical. The child is upset, his heart is racing, breathing becomes shallow, and a message is sent to the brain that there is an emergency. Adrenaline and other stress hormones race through the body, and the child cannot control the outburst. To be fair, adults tantrum too. An adult tantrum simply looks different than a childhood tantrum. A teen or adult who tantrums may slam doors, stamp, and yell at the undeserving people in the room. I have asked children of all ages what adults do when they are frustrated. The responses describe adult tantrums. Students have told me that adults will punch things or yell, throw something, or slam doors. They describe adults who are out of control, but hopefully in a slightly more socially acceptable way than two-year-olds screaming and throwing themselves on the floor.

A preschooler having a tantrum has to go all the way through it. We can try to mitigate tantrums by teaching children to breathe deeply when upset. Deep breaths will keep their hearts from racing so the brain doesn't get a message about an emergency. When we see a child becoming frustrated, we need to encourage the breathing that we have taught.

When we feel ourselves becoming frustrated, we need to practice what we have taught. Having grown up in a generation before the popularity of yoga, meditation, and other very valid Buddhist-based teachings, I have found that I need to actively not only seek the information but open my mind to it. Many of us were raised in a time when these practices would have been written off as nonsense. Unfortunately, it was a time of trauma and great stress that brought me to a place where I realized that I needed to try any tools at my disposal. I remember feeling so unsure and skeptical when someone suggested guided meditation to me. I could not have been more wrong, and I am eternally grateful to have found ways to lead a calmer, less anxious, and far more logical emotional life. I truly believe that not only have I benefited from this emotional intelligence journey but that my students have benefited, too. They are taught by Cindy 2.0—the better Cindy, who knows so much more about her own emotional intelligence and can find ways to impart that knowledge even with very young children.

We always have more to learn about ourselves and our interactions as teachers. Seek the information that either didn't exist during your youth or did exist but you didn't know how to bring it to your classroom. We want our students to be open to possibilities, and we need to do the same.

CHAPTER 7 QUICK NOTES

Set reasonable emotional expectations, remembering:

- Unrelenting happiness is an unrealistic goal.
- All human emotions are normal and acceptable.

Avoid invalidating or offensive statements.

Example	*Do* calmly say and repeat if necessary:	*Don't* say
Sadness	"I see you are sad." Let the child be sad and reassure him with "You will be okay."	"Don't be sad." "Don't cry." "You are being silly."
Fear	"I see you are afraid." Let the child be afraid, and teach courage with "You can be brave and I can help you." "Take a deep breath with me so we can talk about it."	"Don't be scared." "Don't be ridiculous." "You are being silly."
Anger	"I see you are mad." Help the child to calm down with "Take a deep breath with me so we can talk about it."	"Don't be mad." "I don't like when you are mad." "Be a good boy/girl."

Make this your mantra:

- Emotions are normal.
- Our emotions are all acceptable.
- Emotions come and go.
- Emotions are not facts.
- We cannot always control our emotional instincts, but we can control our reactions to them.

Steps to managing emotions:

- What are you feeling?
- Why are you feeling that?
- What can you try?
- What else can you try?
- What was the result?

Mindfulness techniques:

- Deep breathing.
- Engaging senses:
  1. Start by asking very young children to touch something cool such as a tabletop.
  2. Help them to notice the present moment through sensory input, such as: What do you hear? What do you see?

CONVERSATION POINTS WHEN COMMUNICATING WITH PARENTS

- Remind parents that we all experience a range of emotions as part of the human condition, and their children will, too.
- Teach parents to be validating. Tell crying children that they will be okay and scared children that they can be brave, but don't say, "Don't cry," or "Don't be scared."
- Provide parents education about the role that mindfulness, meditation, and other techniques can play both in their own lives, in their ability to parent, and as skills that they can teach their children.
- Explain to parents that their job is to help demonstrate and teach coping mechanisms, not to eradicate unwanted emotions.

CHAPTER **8**

Preschool Classroom Habits: Rethinking Your Routine

"Why?" It is an important question. Preschoolers are so earnest when they ask, "Why?" We asked that question so many times when we were young. In fact, according to Warren Berger's (2014) book, *A More Beautiful Question: The Power of Inquiry to Spark Breakthrough Ideas*, we are at peak questioning age when we are in the preschool years. By the time we enter elementary school, our propensity to ask questions starts a steady downward trend. We stop asking nearly as many questions as we did when we were early learners (Berger, 2014, pp. 43–47). Knowing this should reshape the focus of our approach to learning. We should never stop questioning, and children need to be encouraged more, and with more positivity, to explore curiosity. Too many of our classroom routines are not about their curiosity at all.

Perhaps part of the problem is that we, the adults, haven't questioned as much as a four-year-old for a long time. We have gotten used to being less inquisitive. We need to ask, "Why?" about everything—the behavior of young children, the interactions that we observe, the successes and missteps along our students' path of development, and perhaps most importantly, about our own practices. Why do you teach the lessons that you teach and why do you use certain methodology? Every step of the way, ask yourself, "Why am I doing this the way I am doing it?" "Why" should not be a word owned by or a way of wondering relegated to preschoolers, and then left behind.

We are fortunate to live in a time when we have so much knowledge about how children think and learn. We need to use that knowledge to examine the routines that have been part of early childhood classrooms for many years. Our approach to imparting knowledge needs to be based upon what we have learned over the past several decades and not "just because I've always done that."

Most teachers would agree that we cannot pour our knowledge into the brains of children. Early learners need to discover independently and explore with all their senses. Preschoolers are literal thinkers, who will look for cats and dogs when we say, "It is raining cats and dogs." At the same time, they are magical thinkers who need to experience the bounds of reality to better understand it.

More than anything, they need to care, to be intrigued, and to be an active part of their own learning. Often, when new information is learned and shared about our world, we examine and change our mode of operation. New medical advances bring new treatments. New inventions change our technology. New scientific facts change what and how we teach in our schools. In preschools, however, there are still routines that have remained unchanged by time and knowledge.

It is time to examine and dissect our ways. We need to be willing to refine or retire those routines that no longer make sense. There are activities that we have done for years in early childhood classrooms that do not relate to realistic expectations of young children. In fact, when I point this out to professionals, they have no reason for continuing these older practices and laugh at the notion that these expectations have anything to do with how children learn.

The examination of existing activities must begin with circle time—or what we know really should more accurately be called "group meeting time." Group meeting time is fraught with unrealistic expectations. It is one of my favorite topics to discuss with preschool professionals. I start the discussion with a question: "Why do we force children to sit on the floor?" Time after time, groups of teachers are stymied by that question. I have asked the question for years and am still waiting for an answer that makes sitting on the floor logical. We ask young children who do not yet understand personal boundaries and who have an undeveloped frontal cortex to sit on the floor without touching each other. We have knowledge that negates that expectation. Until the frontal cortex is more developed, young children have trouble controlling impulses (Kim & Lee, 2012).

The children see someone sitting next to them. They have an urge to touch them and so they will. They are sitting on the floor and have an urge to roll around and so they will. We know that part of teaching socialization is helping young children to understand respect for personal boundaries. Then we put them in a situation where there are few or no body boundaries. We want them to pay attention to us, but they are drawn to all the distractions around them. Teachers spend precious moments out of the 10 minutes that children this age might be able to attend to a task saying, "Hands to yourself," "Don't touch her," and "Don't kick." Students are instructed to cross their legs, sit up, and stop rolling around. It's a mess.

Group meeting time is an opportunity to offer our students a chance to make a personal decision. We can offer children choice and dignity by asking how they would like to sit. In my experience, when young children are given the choice between sitting on the floor or sitting in a chair, the majority choose chair. I believe they self-select chair for two basic reasons: They see adults choose to sit in chairs all the time, and their own chair gives them a possession, even if it is for only approximately 10 minutes. I enjoy watching young children bring a chair to group meeting time.

Often, they try to imitate the posture and body positions that they have seen adults use while sitting in chairs. Over the years, I've watched many a child try to cross their ankles, straighten their skirts, or lift the legs of their pants at the inseams, and even try to turn the chair backward to straddle it. They are doing what they have seen adults do when invited to take a seat. They see it as very adult. They imitate the actions of adults. They also will imitate the behavior of an adult. They sit and listen maybe slightly more attentively under this condition, because chair equals a very grown-up way of being.

A chair also provides them with something they lack on the floor. It gives children a physical boundary. When preschoolers sit in chairs, they don't have the opportunity to roll around. They are often less apt to touch each other. They understand the personal space that is outlined by their chair. They also understand the concept of chair. They seem to innately understand that a chair in front of another chair doesn't work well. They start to naturally place chairs next to each other and form an oval.

Giving students the freedom to choose how they will sit is less work for teachers than having to constantly address how they will behave while sitting on the floor. The youngest children, new walkers, in my parent/child classes happily drag their chairs to the gathering area. In fact, they get so used to it that they use chairs to indicate to me when they are ready to sit together and sing.

I will never forget the first time I realized that children who were too young to verbalize their desire to come together for songs were doing so with the chairs. I had been finger painting with a group of parents and their toddlers. I was literally elbow deep in paint. I wanted the children to see that getting paint on my hands or arms didn't hurt me, and actually was fun. I needed more paper and made the mistake of walking near the carpeted group time area. As soon as they saw me move in that direction, the toddlers grabbed chairs and tried to bring them over. They started pulling chairs and grabbing chairs. A couple of the children who were closer to two years old managed to get the chairs by the carpet. They sat down and looked at me expectedly.

With paint all over me, I realized that I needed to start group time. They had communicated that with me. Since that day, I have been involved in numerous activities during parent/child classes with one- and two-year-olds, and watched them drag a chair, sit down, and stare at me. I am always amused, and I always respond to the communication by bringing over a chair and sitting with them.

The children proudly sit in their chairs as soon as they are able. They may not yet be able to sing or clap along, but they sit in those chairs. They can also be taught to put the chairs back at the table. Teachers should use this as an opportunity to teach vocabulary. Rather than just instructing children to put their chairs back, tell them to return their chairs and disperse. They will learn that disperse means to go and spread out if classroom center or playtime follows your group time. If you are headed outside, ask the children to put the chairs by the tables so you can prepare for outdoor play. They will learn that prepare means to get ready.

The first time that you offer children the choice between the floor and a chair, they will not understand that they can really pick one. They will not be used to having an option. When we introduce new choices, it can be confusing. They are so very used to the notion that young children belong on a floor. If your classroom has two adults, you can demonstrate the choice. One of you should sit on the floor while another sits in a chair, and then tell the children that they get to decide. Inevitably, when most children choose a chair, a few will proudly declare their independence from the crowd by saying, "I want to sit on the floor." When we offer this choice or any choice, either option needs to be acceptable. Teachers should not indicate or believe that one option is better than the other. It isn't better to choose sitting on a chair or sitting on the floor. It is simply a personal preference.

The impact of providing students with measurable personal space and the power to make a choice about where to put their own bodies can have a huge impact on the effectiveness of group activities. It will be easier for the students to attend to task. We will have limited the opportunity for distractions. The students will have a more productive and developmentally appropriate experience, so they can enjoy the benefits of their own decision-making process. Once the students are used to selecting a seating preference, the teachers need to determine other ways to make this group gathering more focused on the needs, interests, and developmental level of the children.

The focus of group time shouldn't be about trying to get as much information across in 10 minutes as possible. The information that we try to impart to the entire class at once needs to be age and setting appropriate. A mainstay of the group gathering has traditionally been to teach the concept of time. Calendars make a lovely wall decoration, but the concept of time is not developmentally appropriate for preschool age children. In his study called "The Development of Children's Knowledge of the Times of Future Events," William J. Friedman (2000) showed that four-year-olds' abilities to understand past and future in relation to the present time was inconsistent. He found that five-year-olds were more successful at understanding events that happened in the past or would happen weeks or months in the future. Therefore it is suggested that up to age four the use of the calendar as a measure of time is too abstract for young children to grasp.

We also need to remember that young children view the world from a concrete point of view, with themselves at the center. Children need to care about a concept in order to commit the time to mentally manipulate it and have it become part of long-term memory. A two-, three-, or four-year-old only cares about certain dates and months. Young children care about their birthdays. They care about gift-giving holidays. They care about a day when there will be a special event of interest to them. They do not care that today is Friday. They don't get a paycheck on a certain day of the week like an adult. They care if today is their favorite snack and they don't care that it happens to be Thursday. They care if today is the day the firefighters are coming to visit or the yoga teacher will be at school. They don't understand vague time-related words like "later" or "soon." They care about how many things they will do until they go home.

Our approach to time needs to teach children about measuring it in terms of what they will experience and remembering that they see themselves as the center of the world. Using a classroom calendar to teach children about counting and number recognition is more appropriate than trying to get young children to memorize the date. The time devoted to the topic of time needs to be about the real-life concerns of the average preschooler.

Seek parental permission to take pictures of your students for classroom decorations and charts, and get your camera ready. Each year, take pictures of your current students performing tasks throughout the day. Create cards with their pictures, showing group meeting time, center/playtime, playground time, snack, and the other segments of their day. During your group time, work together each day to put your day in order by placing the cards on the wall in the order in which the day will unfold. The children will learn that time is measured in segments. This is a precursor to teaching minutes, hours, and days. They should also be given the invitation to provide input as to the schedule of the day. They can learn that some events are out of their control. Playground time is assigned. Snacktime may be more flexible. Group meeting time can take place before or after center playtime. By including children in scheduling decisions, they learn about budgeting time. By working on the schedule as a class, they learn about compromise.

For a larger worldview of upcoming and meaningful events, you can go back to the calendar chart. Perhaps a holiday is coming this month, and a classmate will celebrate a birthday. Mark those days with special pictures or symbols. Use those special symbols as signals that we will be counting. Count the number of days until an event. The fact that a birthday is in five days will have little meaning to a preschooler, but it is a good exercise to count with visual clues rather than just aloud by rote. Rote recitation of numbers takes on meaning as the children see the countdown on a chart or calendar, but abstract concepts of time won't be grasped in the preschool years.

When I enter a space for learning, I appreciate knowing the topic and agenda. It puts us at ease when we know what to expect. Afford the same consideration to your young learners. While gathered together, provide them with an oral and visual syllabus for the day. During the typical group time, a teacher might say, "Today, we will learn about the letter C, and we will make birdfeeders."

Play a group game to introduce the concepts and show the students samples of exactly what they will attempt to do. Help the children to be active discoverers of the concepts of the day, rather than passive receivers of scheduling and curricular information. Since they were babies, adults have asked the children to identify pictures. They understand the concept of naming drawings, and it can be a fun game. If you are introducing a new letter, let the children see you drawing pictures of items that start with that letter before your group gathering. If today is about the letter C, for example, sit somewhere in the room and draw a car, a caterpillar, and a cat. Vertical whiteboards or an easel at the children's height are the perfect places to pull up a chair as students are arriving to start to draw. Without saying a word, children will start to stand around you to see what you are doing. Then during your meeting time, you can work together to discover what the pictures have in common—they all start with the letter of the day. Pique the children's interest in today's science exploration by bringing the science tools to the group time area before you ask the children to get a chair or sit on the floor. You can do similar activities prior to your group meeting time that emphasize the crux of the experiences of the day. You may want to draw or create something in front of the students that emphasizes a certain color, shape, number, and so on. Then, when they participate in putting the day's schedule in order, they will understand a little bit about the tasks they are helping to schedule.

The children's confusion about time concepts become evident during conversations. It is common for children who went on a trip sometime in the past to say that they went yesterday. In my experience, to a young child yesterday means any time before right now. Sometimes an incident that happened months ago between two children will be discussed with teachers or parents as if it just happened. More than once, I have had parents ask me about an incident that their child recounted and I have to remind the parents that it happened months ago and not yesterday. Likewise, I have baffled parents by recounting a story their children told us that occurred relatively long ago. We need to give children a sense of the present time by discussing today, a sense of the future by counting to fun events, and a sense of the past by reminding them when something happened long ago. The rest will fall naturally into place as they mature.

Another time-honored but illogical moment during our group gatherings is the discussion that teachers initiate about the weather. There are songs about the weather, charts about the weather, and books about the weather. We do want children to know rain, snow, cold, and warm. The way to know weather is to be in it. We sit in classrooms and talk about the warmth or the fog taking place outside. I can't help but smile when I point out the absurdity of talking about weather indoors every day, and some teachers have shared that they do that in rooms that don't even have windows. Our desire to have children understand weather has been put in a time and place where it doesn't belong. Children who take in the world through their senses need to be feeling, seeing, and smelling the weather live and in person for the information and weather vocabulary to make sense. They can memorize information about weather but being in it sparks more curiosity and deeper learning.

One November, my staff and I decided to teach about both voting and the weather. It was a lesson for us in how young children relate to weather when they aren't standing right in it. We had a weather chart that we cut into pieces. We put the pictures of different weather conditions on a poster board, and each one had a library card pocket. Each child was given a laminated cloud-shaped paper with his or her name on it. We taught the children that when you vote, you put your name by the weather you think is happening today. We showed them that it was sunny, so I put my name in the pocket by the sunny picture. My staff did the same. We told them to put their names by the picture of the weather that they can see out of the classroom windows. Because their clouds had their names on them, we recognized that this crossed the curriculum and also became a literacy/name recognition lesson. We were going to count the votes and integrate math words by determining which condition was allotted more, the most, less, and the least votes. Sometimes, each child would be in the majority but not all the time. We hoped it would be a socialization and teamwork lesson.

From day one, we began to notice interesting responses. It could be 70 degrees and sunny outside, but inevitably a few children would vote for snowy. There was one student during our first year of this activity who really liked to vote for windy. He would actually try to get his classmates to vote for windy. We would find the three-year-old going to his classmates and whispering, "Vote windy" ever so quietly. We began to realize that the inability to separate fact from fantasy and reality from wishes was reflected in their votes. On rainy days, some children would vote for the rain but others voted sunny. Once I asked, "Is it sunny?" and a three-year-old girl replied, "I want it to be sunny." A parent once told me that she saw her son standing by the window at home for a long time. She went to the window to find out what her son was looking at for so long. Finally, one leaf moved and her son said, "There it is. It is windy." The staff and I were triumphant. He understood windy. He had learned that the wind is air that can move leaves. The fact that it wasn't actually what anyone would describe as windy didn't matter.

The children are not little meteorologists. They can't relate to it when they are not in it, and they cannot predict it. If they cannot be in it, we have an obligation to bring it to them. Opening the window for a moment so they can feel the frigid temperatures is a sensory lesson. Going outside in the pouring rain isn't often possible, but the rain can come in. Spray bottles can be used to replicate the conditions outside. Children love being sprayed with water. Adults dislike it, but children love being spritzed. Find inexpensive spray bottles that mist, and you can replicate all sorts of damp conditions. Snow can be brought in. Even fog can be replicated indoors with the purchase of an inexpensive fog machine. A fog machine was one of the best investments I ever made while running a preschool program. We used it to discover that you can run, jump, and crawl through the fog. We learned that the fog outside is made of tiny water drops just like the clouds. The children who have been on airplanes were encouraged to talk about flying through and above the clouds. We can expand that lesson by replicating the water cycle in a sealed, clear sandwich or gallon freezer bag. It is more common to use those bags for planting to see the roots of plants. On occasion, teachers will include a mention of the condensation that forms on the bag as an aside. The evaporation and condensation that will occur inside a clear bag can be available for continued observation, and used as a primary tool when we cannot go out.

Weather should be more than a song. By midway through the year, that perky little weather song slows down. It becomes a part of the routine and no one is learning from it anymore. The tempo slows, along with the enthusiasm. Sing a song if you like, but sing it where it belongs, and with the intention of engaging many different activities to awaken different parts of the brain. Take the children outside to draw or paint the weather. Sit in the weather and start to tell stories about it. Make up a class story about something that happens in that weather. Put containers outside to measure rain and don't forget to go check them after inclement days. Listen for the sounds of the weather. Wind has a sound, as does rain and the lack thereof. Ask the children open-ended questions about what they see, hear, and feel. Sing about what they are feeling and seeing while their senses are fully engaged.

Group time has also traditionally been the time when teachers read to students. The first time that students gather in the morning, they often have much to say. Conversations about the day, the weather, or an introduction to a book can easily be thwarted by a student who needs to talk about the weekend with grandma or time at an amusement park. It is important that children have the opportunity to say what they are thinking about, remembering, and processing. If they are thinking about it, they have difficulty with resisting the urge to talk about it.

I've had staff members who shortened the name of the gathering of students in their classroom from group meeting time to group. They started simply saying, "It's time for group." A few parents laughingly commented to me that it sounds like therapy. I told them, "Well, it is like therapy. Your children will get a chance to talk about what is on their minds." We might also spend some of that time considering behavior, much like in a therapist appointment. If the children tend to fight over one particular toy or there is always the same behavioral issue on the playground, group meeting time can be when we calmly discuss the problem and children can offer solutions.

Books are portable and can be read anytime of the day but those important thoughts—the stories they cannot wait to tell us—need to be released from their brains. A child who wishes to engage in public speaking should not be stopped because of an adult's agenda. They can learn to wait to take their turn to speak, but they should be given a turn and not asked to wait until everyone has dispersed. Their own stories provide such wonderful opportunities to promote conversational and critical thinking skills.

Grasp the opportunity to ask the question that we are asked most often: "Why?" When a student needs to share that he went to grandma's house, ask "Why did you go to grandma's house?" When a student needs to tell you that she went to the zoo, inquire why she went there. When children are asked why about their own stories, they really need to think for a moment. Sometimes, young people will say that they went because their parents took them. Good enough! Other times, they may say that they don't know why they went there. That's a fine answer, too. The question will get them to think about their days, and that is the goal—to expand the conversation and the critical thinking process. When we tell a story, we know that people are listening and interested when they ask us a question about the tale. The same is true for children. They will know you are paying attention and that you care. Group time should be for sharing thoughts and ideas.

If conversations ensue, be willing to put your book aside. Group gathering times can happen more than once per day. There are other times when children are gathered and books would be a great way to keep them entertained. Plan to read when children are waiting. Read while they are waiting for time on the playground or for tables to be cleaned for snack. On occasion, read during snacktime as a treat. Reading makes a great transition from one part of the day to another. It doesn't need to be the star of the group-time show. It can, however, be used to set a cooperative and calm tone during what can be more stressful moments for the children. Transitions are stressful but reading is calming.

When we do read to children, we need to watch for clues about their level of interest in the book. Adults have a need to finish books even when children are not listening. It is entirely possible that the book you selected isn't nearly as captivating as you predicted. When I present to groups of teachers, we laugh at our need to finish the book even when no one else cares. This is especially true of those fancy books with pop-ups and tabs. Teachers love pop-up books. Let's be honest—we are intrigued. I cannot figure out how they fold the paper just so and the picture pops up every time. Stand in a bookstore aisle where there are pop-up books or even books with tabs to pull, and you will see adults picking them up with fascination. Children also want to touch them but, alas, they rarely are permitted to do so. We store those books out of the reach of children because they may rip the tabs and three-dimensional pictures, especially if they are on a quest to determine how the book works. The books are a curiosity, and we don't allow for it. It is not realistic to assume that children will be interested in something they are not permitted to explore with their senses. We need to admit when the book is a flop or the fancy tabs are a tease. I have watched the same scene over and over. A teacher is holding a pop-up book and repeatedly saying to the children, "Look. Look at this." The teacher has to tell the children to look because, well, they aren't looking. If they aren't looking, they aren't as interested as we wish.

We want to encourage a love of the written word, not have a boring or frustrating experience. If they are not listening, stop reading. You can check out that fascinating pop-up book on your own time, because, through their actions, the children who are looking around the room and interacting with each other have told you that they aren't interested.

During group meeting times, we can even learn a bit about coping skills. We can use this calm gathering time to learn about relaxation and how to relax our bodies. While the class is calm, and listening, we can learn to tune into our physicality. Instead of trying to teach concepts that they are not developmentally ready to learn, use your gathering to teach about breathing. Yoga and meditation are all the rage today because everyone is so stressed. When you learn about yoga and meditation, you learn that it is all about breathing, because deep breaths calm the brain and even promote brain growth. In 2012, the American Institute of Stress posted an article that stated, "Abdominal breathing for 20 to 30 minutes each day will reduce anxiety and reduce stress. Deep breathing increases the supply of oxygen to your brain and stimulates the parasympathetic nervous system, which promotes a state of calmness. Breathing techniques help you feel connected to your body—it brings your awareness away from the worries in your head and quiets your mind" (American Institute of Stress, 2012). It is true for all ages, children and adults. Teaching about breathing and being able to calm the body is the most important item on a group-time agenda.

When you are not gathered together, it is an appropriate expectation that children will want to explore and experiment. When they leave group time and spread out among the many activities in the room, it is inappropriate to squash that desire, even when we perceive their actions as messy or unorganized. Their own explorations propel them toward a greater understanding of the world. Just as we should allow children to mix colors of Play-Doh, we need to let them go to the art area and mix the paint. We need to let them pour sand out of the sand table so they can see it hit the floor. They learn from watching the sand hit the floor and bounce around. It is unrealistic to expect that they won't keep trying to get that sand out of the table if they are curious about it. Rather than fight the curiosity tide, teachers need to consider how they can allow for the activity.

All this mixing, pouring, and the inevitable dumping of toys will create quite a mess. When I ask teachers their reasons for restricting the mixing of materials or the number of toys on the shelves, they reluctantly admit that they set those limits because of the potential mess. A preschool classroom should be a mess. If I walk into a classroom in the middle of the day and no one has to tell me to watch my step, something is amiss. It is wonderful to walk over to a sand table and find rice from the other sensory area it in. That means the children were curious about putting the rice in the sand and that someone allowed the exploration. When parents toured a school that I directed, I always told them, "I know you are shopping around. If you see a preschool that doesn't have this sort of mess, question the goals, focus, and discipline methods of that school."

Young children should have the freedom to move from one item to another and then come back. Have you ever started reading the mail and put it down on the table to investigate a noise outside? This is no different than building with blocks, hearing something interesting from another group of children, and going to investigate. Something catches our attention and we put the mail on the table. Something catches a child's attention and the child walks away from the blocks. Sometimes we go right back to the mail and sometimes we don't. We might go back hours later. In the meantime, we have created a mess on the table. We have left something there that doesn't belong. It is unrealistic to expect children to constantly put everything away. We need to understand that cleaning up has to be factored into our time schedules. Cleanup time becomes fraught with unrealistic expectations when we sing about it, repeatedly tell children to clean up, and think that they will follow all the required steps.

Cleanup is a huge task. In "Bring Out The Best In Your Children," the American Academy of Pediatrics (2014) gives two pieces of advice that are in direct conflict to how cleanup time is conducted in most classrooms. The Academy advises that instructions given to children be stated simply. They suggest that we use the children's age as a guideline. Directions given to a two-year-old should be two words, three-year-olds should be given three-word directives, and so on. They also state that we need to focus only on up to three goals at one time. Think about the sentences we use for cleanup and the steps that those two words encompass. To clean up the room, the children have to pick up a toy, determine where it goes, put it there, come back, and get another one. It is at least a five-step process. It is overwhelming. I ask adults, "When you are overwhelmed, what do you do?" They reply, "Shut down," or "I do nothing." The same is true for young children who are told to clean up. It is too much for them to compute. When the task is overwhelming, the children will walk around the room without picking things up. They are shutting down. They may put one thing away and then do something else. They whirl around the room and teachers state the obvious, "You aren't picking anything up." Teachers sing encouraging songs, but they are just that—songs. Much as the ABC song doesn't really teach an understanding of letters and their use, the songs about cleaning up don't teach the task. The students dance. They sing. The toys are still on the floor. In every class, there is a student who is a master cleaner-upper. That student thrives from having things in their place and from the positive attention he gets from putting them there. It is a sad state of affairs when one student is running here, there, and everywhere while the others sing, dance, and whirl, but the teacher is just glad the toys are being put on the shelves. It is the teacher's job to find a way to motivate students to participate in cleaning up just as much as it is our job to motivate them to embrace literacy activities. It is fine for the great cleaner-upper to be the captain of that activity, but we need to figure out how to make it less daunting for the others. The classroom is their community too, and they have a responsibility to maintain the community. Cleaning up is more of an overarching life lesson than we often realize.

We cannot expect to stand in a room and have the majority of early childhood learners able to follow the multistep directive that is implicit in the words "clean up." In this situation and many others, we use too many words and we are often the source of loss of focus. We know that young, egocentrically based thinkers have to care, so we try to motivate them by setting a goal that has nothing to do with the task at hand. Often, teachers can be heard saying, "Clean up so we can go outside." It is always amusing to watch young children react to that confusing goal message. The goal is really to clean up the room, but the adult has stated that the goal is to get outside. It is no wonder that the children will run for their coats while the toys remain strewn around the floor.

If the goal is to pick up the toys from the floor, we need to conduct an activity that keeps that at the center. We know that children learn best through play, respond well when they care, and need to be having fun. We need to have games that get children to clean up just like we have games to engage their senses, attract them to literacy skills, and expand their understanding of nature.

There are three magic, motivating words in the preschool years: ready, set, go. The children love to "ready, set, go." They need to race to a measurable goal. Pick a song that the children know and tell them that you will sing it. The toys must be picked up and put in their place before you finish the song. If it is a song they know, they can predict the end. "Ready, set, go!" and you start singing. They will run around the room, picking up toys and tossing them on the shelves. Will the toys all be put exactly in the right bin? No, but that wasn't your goal. Your goal was to get them off the floor. Later, you can teach sorting by asking children to find toys in the wrong bin and put them where they belong. Sorting and cleanup are actually two separate activities. "Pick the toys up" is four words, but one directive. "Put all the toys in their correct places," is something else entirely. Remember, the children are coming back later or tomorrow, and the toys will get mixed up again. It is more important to pick things up than to sort them when you have a strict time constraint. The sorting can become part of the picking up if the bins are placed near the appropriate toys. It's a bit of suggestive selling to our students—the bins are around you, so maybe you can find the right one. If your goal, however, is simply to get the stuff off the floor, then stick to the one goal until it becomes too easy for them to beat the time of the song.

When they consistently win the time race, then add the next directive. Change the game. The new game is that they must pick up and put the toys in the right place. It is akin to when adults follow a new recipe. The first few times we bake, we need the recipe in front of us to follow every individual step. Bake the item often enough, and you may be able to follow the first steps without referring to the recipe. Eventually, you memorize all the steps and don't need the written recipe at all. Cleanup is a recipe. Step by step, one at a time, they will be able to do more without going back to the recipe if we let them memorize the tasks a little at a time.

As we reconsider our perception and our approach regarding cleanup, we need to examine the notion that every single item must be put away multiple times per day. Why does everything have to be put away before every transition? I have been in classrooms and watched the multiple cleanups—before circle time, before snack, before going outside, before lunch. We act as if they aren't coming back to play again in less than 30 minutes. If we acknowledge that the time to clean up has everything to do with our adult need for some sort of order and little to do with the students' completion of exploration, then we need to determine what we can do to allow the children to decide if they will be coming back to the toy. They should have the right to finish what they started. Imagine your frustration if you started a jigsaw puzzle and someone came into the room and said, "Tough luck. Time to put it away." Then you started it again and after another segment of time you were asked to stop and put it away once more. How frustrating! I wonder how frustrating our consistent commands to clear the room are for our students.

Children need to learn to determine when they are done using an item. We need to dictate it far less than has been traditionally done. When children learn to consider their own "doneness" or their own completion of a task, the massive classroom cleanup becomes much less eventful, and even unnecessary. Children should be taught to think about their own use of classroom objects. Instead of directing children to clean up, we should be asking children, "Are you done?" It stops them in their tracks. They have to think and consider. When we see children walking away from a toy or activity, there is no reason to wait for the group cleanup time. We should kindly inquire, "Are you done with that?" If the child says yes, we need to teach a lesson in respect for property and people. We need to tell them that when they are done it goes back on the shelf so someone else can use it. Putting one thing away is also far less overwhelming than asking them to look at a room filled with objects and to put them all away. If the student says that he is not done, we need to model respect for that decision and self-determination by having a system by which the objects can be left out for a while.

The best activities cross the curriculum, and cleanup can cross into a name recognition and literacy activity. The children should have the right to label a toy for later use, and they can do that with name recognition activities. Each child can have a name tag to place on materials that should not be cleaned up yet. When the child indicates that she is not done with the items, the name tag is placed on them. The children will learn that this means that someone is coming back, so please don't put it away. By allowing children to decide if they are done, the act of putting items away becomes more self-regulating. When you introduce this concept, talk to the students before they are in the situation. Show them their name tags and how to place them on the item they would like to use again. Use your group time to demonstrate this new concept. Explain that they will each have one name tag that can be placed on one thing to go back to when they return. To make this an independent activity, the name tags should be within the children's reach. Eventually, after many days of guidance, they will be able to get the name tags, tag an activity, and know what that means without your help. Name tags can be designed a number of ways—name only, name and photo of the child, name and illustration by the child. The important messages are not about the specific method for creating the tag but about choice, independence, and respect.

Children find comfort from this and other routines. Predictable days are a comfort to us all. Surprises, both good and bad, can be behaviorally disturbing. We get knocked off course, and children don't have the tools to respond to that change. It is important to be as predictable as possible, but we do need to consider what is routine in our days. Merriam-Webster's online dictionary defines routine as a "regular way of doing things in a particular order" and "a boring state or situation in which things are always done the same way." Activities in a particular order is good. Actions as a matter of rote and as part of a boring state are not. Bore the children, and you lose the teachable moments of curiosity seeking.

"Why am I doing this?" needs to be a constant refrain when planning your days. "What does this actually teach?" rather than "What do I wish it teaches?" needs to be the backdrop for that question. Ask yourself, "What measurable knowledge do I observe the children learning from this activity?" If you ask, "Why this routine?" and your answer is, "It's always been done this way," then you need to look for better, more intriguing and effective ways to reach your specific goals. Sorry, weather song—you are boring us. You are not teaching the feel of the weather. You've got to go.

CHAPTER 8 QUICK NOTES

Improve your group time:

- Let children choose between sitting on the floor or in a chair.
- Create a living daily schedule calendar by taking your students' photos doing each of the typical day's activities and have them help you place that in order each morning.
- Before your group meeting time, pique the students' interest by drawing objects that emphasis the crux of today's lesson. Let students observe your drawing, and use that curiosity to help create an oral syllabus for the day.
- Save weather discussions for when you are outside, or at least by a window.
- Allow the students to talk about what is on their minds.
- If you are reading and the children aren't interested, stop. You can try to revisit the book later.
- Use this calm time to teach deep breathing and other coping techniques.

Encourage children to learn about their world freely:

- Remember that children are curious about dumping and spills. Let them see what happens to satisfy their curiosity.

- Let children discover what happens when they mix and match, including paint, dough, and solid substances such as rice and sand.

Have realistic cleanup expectations and goals:
- Make cleanup time matter by making it fun. Play a game that makes cleanup a race.
- Keep directives short and specific.
- Be clear about your goal and the steps you need to teach:

  1. Your first goal is to get the toys off the floor. Sorting can be done later.
  2. Once the children consistently pick toys up, change the game to include putting items in their place.

- Allow the possibility that the children may want to come back to what they have started. Allow them to determine if they are done.

Question your own routines by asking yourself:
- Why am I doing this?
- What does this actually teach?
- What measurable knowledge do I observe the children learning from this?
- Why is this part of my routine?

CONVERSATION POINTS WHEN COMMUNICATING WITH PARENTS

- Parents are used to seeing certain activities that we now know aren't effective learning experiences (such as teaching calendar). Explain to parents that we now know that rote learning is not as valuable as once thought. Better learning occurs when children are actively engaging their senses and our lessons are meaningful.

- Guide parents in questioning their interactions, too. Make this the Year of Questioning Our Interactions—are they meaningful to the children, or are we all just doing what was done with us? Make it a school-wide quest for better learning. When parents understand and are involved in change, they may find it to be more valuable and acceptable.

- Remind parents that all of us can only follow a maximum of a few steps at a time, so our directions to the children need to be step-by-step and specific.

CHAPTER **9**

Sheep Aren't Made of Cotton Balls: The Importance of Self-Expression

A group of pre-K students had been given precut pieces of houses. They had a roof, home, windows, and door. As often is the case, I couldn't resist asking them a question: "What are you doing?" The answer was one that I have heard over and over from students: "Gluing." They told me that they were gluing. They did not say that they were making a house. I didn't correct them because they had accurately told me what they were doing. They hadn't created the pieces, and they were told to glue. There was nothing artistic about the activity. Using glue does not make it art.

Every day and throughout the day, preschool students should be given opportunity for self-expression. Young children need to create their own pieces of art, write their own books, and explore the world without unsolicited adult intervention. When adults precut paper and tell young children where to glue it, they are not participating in an art activity. That is a lesson in following directions and gluing. Sheep are not made of cotton balls, but for years, preschoolers have glued cotton balls onto paper to create facsimiles of sheep. Those cotton balls are not what sheep are made of, and everyone in the room knows it. In today's technological era, we don't need to pretend that those cotton-ball-filled pieces of construction paper teach children about sheep. We can pull technology right out of our pockets and show them real sheep. Children who are learning about sheep should have the opportunity to observe the real thing and then represent them in art however they choose. Parents who see a room full of identical art should be concerned about the teaching methods being practiced. Twenty identical sheep made of cotton balls is not evidence of thinking, considering, evaluating, creating, and learning.

When children have to create from scratch, it ignites the brain. It is the job of the educator to expand their thinking and their capacity to be analytical. The more we limit their choices, the less their thinking is expanded. The more involved we are in the activity, the less they have to stretch their thinking. When we hand a student the four legs, body, mane, and head of a horse precut from paper and tell them where to glue it all, they don't need to think. We also lose an opportunity to see what stage of development each child has reached. Evidence that art reflects growth and learning is apparent when watching a young child draw. Consider the evolution of their development that is evident when they try to draw humans. First, they draw only a huge circle. Two years later, they draw a person with a body and arms. Their perceptions are being refined, and their fine motor skills are improving. It is fascinating to watch artistic abilities develop. Seemingly random circles and blobs of paint are followed by pictures that take more form. Someday, those pictures will be evidence of what each child was able to do at ages two, three, and four years old. What the teacher is able to do when the children are four years old shouldn't be a part of the equation. The teacher can obviously cut a straight line and recognizable shapes, and glue them in place. Direct that activity over and over with 20 children and all we have is what an adult could do when the children were four years old.

When you precut, suggest placement, and create identical works, you are not doing art. We need to be clear about the goal of the activity. When you precut and are directing children, you are asking them to participate in a craft that teaches cognitive skills. Cognitive skills are important but they are too often confused with art. One of my favorite cognitive projects for the theme "springtime" is to create a counting kite. I help the children trace or draw a diamond, a long rectangle, and several short rectangles. I ask the children to cut on the lines. Some do better than others, of course. Because cutting is a skill that needs to be honed as fine motor skills improve, I am happy to help the students by turning the paper or using two-person scissors. Once the pieces are cut, we work together to create a kite by identifying the shapes and gluing them together. The tail of the kite needs to be long enough for a number of short rectangular strips to be added. The strips are wide enough to write one number on each strip and draw items to match the number. A strip might have a number 3 on it so I ask the student to draw 3 things of their choice. We put the strips in numerical order and glue them on the tail. The children have identified shapes and numbers, and counted. The completed piece looks like a kite, but it was not that day's art activity. It was a craft that taught math, fine motor, and other skills. It was a craft because I had a particular product in mind. There was another activity available for freely creating that day and every day. Art is what the children have created themselves. Art is completely open ended with no pre-determined product or outcome.

Art should be at the core of our intentional teaching because it helps to develop confident decision-making skills. Students should be able to choose if they will create with markers, crayons, paint, or another medium. When teachers decide for them, the activity is not self-expression. Realistically, we tend to theme teach, and want to encourage children to create a drawing or painting based upon our theme, or the book we read. Teachers can make suggestions, but know that art on a different topic shouldn't be deemed wrong. Most young children, when shown a picture of a dog, will take the suggestion to paint or draw one. Others may smile at you and paint grandma's house. We learn from that, too. It doesn't mean that the child is incapable of following your directions or wasn't paying attention. It means that the most important topic to that child at that moment is grandma's house. The world won't end because that child didn't draw the dog.

We also need to know ourselves and teach others that preschoolers' art is not a reflection of their knowledge about vocabulary. It is not a means for determining if their knowledge of words includes a connection to actual objects. A child might take her favorite color of paint, make a big blob with the paintbrush, and declare that she has painted a car. Just because her painted car isn't recognizable to us doesn't mean she is incapable of going to the parking lot and accurately identifying a car. Details emerge as development progresses. Eventually tires will be added to that blob, but not today.

We learn so very much when children are true self-expressive artists. We learn about their view of their families when they are simply allowed to draw them. It is interesting to note if the people they draw depict emotion and have smiles. We learn about how they view themselves and their other family members as part of the group by their sizes and positions on the paper. I am always fascinated when children draw themselves at the same height as their parents. I wonder if it speaks to the style of parenting that the child has drawn everyone on an even scale.

Without commenting to the students, we can observe their worldviews. We learn about how they believe that anything can happen when they draw the sky and the grass with unlikely colors. We watch as their thinking becomes more reality based when that sky becomes always blue in their drawings. When we allow them to select paint or markers, we learn their developmental preference between long, sweeping motions with a brush and more precise line work with a writing tool. Predraw, precut, and instruct exactly how to create a piece, and the teacher has lost such valuable opportunities to understand the thinking and developmental levels of her students. Every day, child-created art and a variety of materials need to be simply other activity options in your room.

The easels in the classroom should always be stocked with paint and available to the students. Markers, crayons, colored pencils, and a variety of paper should be within reach. Children should self-select time to draw and paint, just as they self-select time to build with blocks or play dress-up. Self-selection itself is a form of self-expression.

The children in my classes have always been used to freely choosing art materials whenever they wish. It is true for all ages. One day, a group of almost two-year-olds arrived, and the paint was not at the easel. The child-safe containers had been removed for cleaning, and we forgot to get them from the sink in another room. The children were perplexed. They stood at the easels. They looked at us. They put their hands in the holes that usually held the paint cups. We could see the confusion on their faces. We couldn't help but be interested in their reactions. They made it obvious that the lack of opportunity to self-select the paint at the easels was an issue. We were sorry to have upset the children, but look at what they learned! They knew that they had this choice. It was a normal part of the routine to simply paint, and they didn't need to ask. We quickly retrieved the materials, set them up, and the children were so happy.

Literacy activities provide another opportunity for students' self-expression and a glimpse at their thinking. Children who are allowed to freely be storytellers, authors, and illustrators get to explore literacy rather than just observe it. Preschoolers create stories all the time when they pretend. We unfortunately fail to capitalize on this. The worlds they create at the dollhouse or dress-up or when they build are not separate from meaningful literacy work. They are integral parts of early literacy. Dramatic play areas are the creative and oral story centers in classrooms. It is where literacy skills begin. When you watch a typically developing child at play, you can practically see how much he is thinking. Listen carefully. Children often talk aloud when immersed in play. If no one is there, they will talk to themselves as they create stories for their cars, dolls, or structures. Those oral stories can become pieces of art and literature if we encourage children to create from their own experiences.

In a typical early childhood classroom, teachers are at tables with students doing crafts and literacy on paper. Students are around the room designing new worlds. Rarely do the activities around the room connect to the activities at the table. Teachers need to offer students a way to take their imaginative work and make it the focus of more creations. When children are playing dress-up, for example, ask them what they are pretending. What is the story? Offer the children a chance to draw and write about their own imaginative stories as often as you do about stories that other people have published.

The confidence students can gain from early positive experiences with self-expression will help to carry them through so many facets of the years to come. Think about what we are praising when a young child traces a line that we have drawn for them. When we have done the bulk of the work and we say, "Good line!" we are saying, "You followed instructions well," which to a young child really interprets something like, "You did what I wanted you to do well." Following instructions is an important skill. It has its place but it needs to be balanced with acknowledgment of and time for the children's creative thinking and individual abilities. Just as early learners are just discovering where their bodies end and other people's begin, they need to know how it feels to have original thoughts and that their own thoughts have value.

I walked into a classroom holding my smartphone because my skirt didn't have pockets. I asked the three-year-olds what we could sing. One lovely girl requested the theme song from her favorite television show. I told her that I don't know that song and she aptly pointed out that my phone knows it. She asked me to find it on my smartphone. I asked the student to sing the words herself, but she didn't know them. She repeated the request to find the song on my phone. I told her that I would like to sing a song that she just knows, not watches. She was stumped. The three-year-old didn't understand that there was a difference between what the world put out and what she knew. Ordinarily, I wouldn't show video during preschool but I thought this was an important, teachable moment. I looked up her request and showed it to the group of children who had now gathered around. They all knew this children's show and they loved watching the song. As soon as it was over, I said, "Now let's sing a song without a video." I suggested "Itsy Bitsy Spider." They joyfully sang and did the accompanying hand motions. I told them, "That was a song that you have in your brain," and I pointed to my head. I said, "Your brain is in your head and it remembers things and it makes up wonderful things. Can you make up a song from your brain?" The girl who had requested the video began to sing her own song. We celebrated the things we know and can make with our brains. We laughed. We high-fived. Several times after that when I was in the classroom, I heard young students talking about something they knew from their brains. We continued to praise their knowledge and creations. They rejoiced in what came from their brains while painting and singing. They had their first lesson in the joy of self-expression.

They also had a lesson in the difference between the limitless things they can create vs. the limitations of what is already created. I noticed that when they made up songs, they were long. They didn't always make sense to me and, often, the same few sentences were repeated over and over. When I listen closely, I hear songs about their toys, pets, and favorite places. Sometimes, I listen to their renditions of their favorite songs over and over. They discover that what they can do, think, sing, and create has no limits. Innovators, inventors, and great storytellers push the lines of limitation to give to the world things that are completely new. Look around your classroom. These children could be the next innovators, inventors, and great storytellers. On occasion, we should take a moment to realize that and to note how lucky we are to be a part of a profession that touches the future. If we really want to touch the future, we have to foster the children's belief in their own unique abilities to create.

In an environment where there is no right and wrong to self-expression and time is allotted for it, we lay a foundation for a positive self-identity. Erikson taught that in the preschool years, a child's identity is shaped by two struggles. First, a child wrestles with the struggle between autonomy, and shame and doubt (McLeod, 2013). A young child realizes he can do things without an adult's assistance. He can make a decision. He can paint or draw or sing songs on his own. Activities centered on self-expression help children to have those moments of autonomy when they can create independently, and there is no shame or doubt because there is no wrong answer. Whatever is painted is worthy. That is so different than when an adult corrects the poorly traced line or the incorrect number counting. Next, Erikson said that children struggle with initiative vs. guilt (McLeod, 2013). This is when children become creators. They walk over to the blocks and make a structure with no instructions. They mold the Play-Doh and draw a picture however they wish. They are taking initiative and need to understand the feeling of pride in their own efforts. When a child picks up a marker and writes on a wall instead of on a more appropriate place, the adults will correct her. Self-expression allows children the time and space to take the initiative without chance for guilt. There will be enough times in the years ahead when initiative will not be applauded. Many times children stand at crossroad having to decide if their own efforts have merit. They wonder if they should attempt to be original or different. When a three- or four-year-old knows that their efforts have value and they can rely on their own thoughts, knowledge, and imagination, they have been taught that they themselves have value.

During a typical day, there will be crafts that are being created to support teacher-led curriculum. If the theme of the week is in the fall, you can be sure that preschoolers are cutting, tracing, and/or coloring different colored leaves. If a holiday is coming, crafts are being introduced to support teaching symbols and values from those holidays. There are many schools that ensure there is time for what they call "free" art. "Free" means free from directives from adults, "free" from having to be about a theme or a concept introduced by adults, and "free" from being a required detail in the curriculum. Unfortunately, there are times when teachers will forgo the free art because there isn't time or space and it doesn't seem as important as the craft that is derived from the book we read. If in our lesson plans, curricular descriptions, and goal statements, we started to call this "self-expression," it might be viewed more seriously and there could be more recognition for the added skill practice time. When we put paper on an easel and children paint blobs, they don't look important to us, but time at that easel was essential. Easel work helps to strengthen the fine motor muscles. When children cut paper into tiny tidbits that fall on the table and the floor, adults simply wonder if that can be easily cleaned up with a broom. Actually, the time with the scissors is building muscles that promote development of the pincer grip. Children who tell their stories and are expressing themselves through oral language are honing their literacy skills.

Time for self-expression is time for important skill development. Give this time the respect it deserves by calling it "self-expression"—an accurate, adult phrase that is less likely to "freely" be skipped, or abbreviated when time feels short. Self-expression should be listed with literacy, math, and other typical subject areas in your lesson plans. The difference is in the planning. Plan for self-expression not through detailed adult-created ideas, but by listing the ways in which students will have opportunities for self-expression. For example, you might write a lesson plan that says, "Children will freely choose paint, crayons, markers, and paper to draw," or "Children will be encouraged to draw, dictate thoughts to teachers, or . . ." Then, as my son often says when I question what will be, just let it happen.

CHAPTER 9 QUICK NOTES

Art is a means of observing development and encouraging confident decision-making skills.

- Children need to create from scratch.
- Active creation is evidence of thinking, considering, evaluating, and learning.
- Children need to choose their own art subjects and materials every day.

Literacy is a means of self-expression.

- Dramatic play is the creative and oral story center of the classroom.
- Connect dramatic play to more literacy development by asking children to retell the pretend story through drawing, dictation, and other means of written expression.
- Add a category in your lesson plans called "self-expression" to give it the same weight and consideration as literacy, math, and other typically lesson-planned subject areas. That category shouldn't include student instructions—it should simply say that children will freely be able to express themselves through art, dictation, and so on.

CONVERSATION POINTS WHEN COMMUNICATING WITH PARENTS

- Teach parents about the importance of self-expression. It is through self-expression that we get a window into the child's skill level, worldview, and sense of self.
- Help parents to understand that children need to make choices in order to become confident decision makers.

- Explain that precut and highly instructive projects are for cognitive learning and are not art.
- Help parents to understand that young children are creators, and we can encourage them to keep creating if we allow for self-expression.

CHAPTER **10**

Readiness for Reading and Writing: Observing the Development of the Whole Child

When students of my generation were in kindergarten, we played and finger painted. We learned to recognize our names, to function as a class, and to feel competent in the absence of our parents. It wasn't very long ago, but it seems so because of the changes in our society. When I went to kindergarten, I was one of the very few students who had attended a preschool program. Preschool was not a staple yet in the United States. We also didn't have as many things—toys, possessions, technology—and were therefore less product focused.

The focus on product rather than process has opened the door for more standardized testing and more emphasis on the importance of what testing measures. The world has changed. The result of increased preschool education and a focus on product rather than process has impacted our early childhood settings. In the United States, children start formal reading lessons earlier. They are asked to write at younger ages. The curriculum has taken a tumble downward. What was taught in second grade is now part of the first-grade curriculum. Kindergarten students are being taught lessons that used to start in first grade. Everywhere I go and lecture, teachers bemoan the falling down of the curriculum, particularly in the area of literacy. Some have pointed out that they have observed a two-year fall-down of curriculum, and what used to be second-grade work can now be observed in some kindergartens. The carefree days of finger painting and playing through kindergarten are over, and are perceived as acceptable for only the youngest of our preschoolers but not for children entering the pre-kindergarten year. The pre-kindergarten students begin to feel the effects of this era when we start to demand more production on paper from them. They are being asked to begin reading and writing younger than in prior generations and often before they themselves are developmentally ready.

Early literacy has become a main focus in our preschools. Preschool administrators and teachers feel pressure, and in some cases dread, that their schools won't measure up to the ever-increasing demand for more evidence of learning at younger ages. Why is pressure being focused so keenly on preschools? Adults like to have measurable results and to have learning look like their memories of being students. Reading and writing are tangible and relatable to adults. Our last learning experiences were very literacy based. We sat in high school or college classrooms and wrote. We wrote notes. We wrote essays. We wrote answers to tests and agonized through the writing of research papers. Literacy is at the crux of all subjects of the curriculum. We read books. We carried books. We used books to learn facts and to find information. Adults remember the judgment of their knowledge being based on the written word or the spoken word, and sometimes a combination of the two during the oral report. We remember that our own success depended on our ability to read and write, and so adults put a great deal of emphasis on the literacy component of any curriculum. It is especially true of today's world that we are product based, and when we see young children read and write, we feel that a desired product has been produced.

There seems to be a belief that there is benefit to children learning to read and write earlier. Studies are published supporting this belief as well as decrying it. In the end, for individual children, the debate is a moot point. Every child develops at a different rate. The ability to read and write depends upon the coordination of the development of the brain and of the body. We cannot force children who are not ready to read or write. Trying to force a child to read or write before being developmentally ready serves only to defeat that child. It is counterproductive. The child who cannot properly hold the pencil struggles. The child who isn't ready for the extended thinking process that a letter makes a sound and that they combine to make a word is frustrated by attempts to read. Typically developing children will get there. The educational dilemma is how we address pressure from worried parents and a demanding public education system, and still preserve the students' feelings of self-worth and capability, while encouraging their growth and a love of literacy.

Knowing that so much of a child's future education will depend on their affinity for and abilities in the area of literacy, educators need to be both well informed about the facts of learning literacy and the impact our approach has on our students' perceptions about reading and writing. If we make it a defeating chore at age three or four, we have set the children up for trouble in the future. The societal pressures on educators cannot force us into a position of doing the wrong thing for children. We need to seek more and more knowledge about how children develop and how we can encourage the development of muscle skills and brain pathways. That is not synonymous with putting pencils in hands that aren't ready or trying to get children to repeat meaningless sounds. It is our job to gather relatable facts to teach people the appropriate expectations of literacy development. We don't expect high school students to succeed in a physics class before they have passed algebra. We know that math skills need to be developed and taught before they can succeed in physics class. The same is true for reading and writing. We need to ensure that other skills have developed first.

There are concrete signs that a child is ready to write and to read. When you work in the field of early childhood education for many years, you learn to spot the signs that your students are ready to read and write almost by instinct. Unfortunately, we do a poor job of communicating to parents that nearly every preschool activity leads to all the skills students need to acquire before they can sound out words and write letters. Educators need to take a step back and think about the purpose of what we ask children to do during play. We need to help others see how literacy skills will not develop without the muscle growth that comes from our crafts, activities of self-expression, dramatic play time, and other fun and games.

An Internet search of "reading and writing readiness" will produce lists of skills and activities that children need to master to succeed in early literacy. The search provides the list of pre-writing shapes that a child has to master, the gross and fine motor muscles that need to develop, and the coordination that needs to be honed between both hemispheres of the brain. Our challenge as early childhood educators is to take that readily available information and apply it by intentionally providing activities that help encourage our students' development. We also need to recognize that we must teach parents who are so afraid that their children won't succeed as adults if they spend time with the scissors or crafts or dress-up toys when they are young. Their children are, in fact, setting the path to reading and writing one building block at a time.

From the time children are babies, adults sing the ABC song with them. Toddlers arrive at preschool for their first day familiar with that song. When teachers sing it during their group meeting time in the first few weeks, the very young children stare at them as if to say, "How do you know that song that my parents and grandparents have been singing for me?" The ABC song is a great tool for teachers to use to build a bridge between the children's two most important worlds. It is, however, merely a song. It provides us with the same bridge to home as so many other common songs and stories. When children hear it at their school and at home, they begin to recognize that the things they do at home and at school are not restricted to one setting or the other. All learning applies to functioning in the whole world. The ABC song is one of the first long pieces of information that children memorize. It is great brain exercise, but again it is just a song. It is not teaching them alphabet in the way they need to understand it for future literacy. We can hear that it is, to the children, just a song when the "L-M-N-O-P" section becomes not letters but more random sounds. That section of the song is always a mess when children first learn it. Some children also think that the second-to-last letter of the song is "and," as in "y and z." They are imitating, memorizing, and repeating. They are not learning the meaning and function of letters when they simply sing. The song goes so quickly that it is not an easy task to slow it down to point to letters as they sing.

Time is better spent trying to create familiarity with the letters when we are not singing the ABC song. The alphabet memorized in order is not the goal. Words have our letters in all sorts of combinations, and so children need to also recognize letters in random order.

Most people know to start showing children that letters make words by showing them their own names. At some point, seeing their own names will matter to them. When a child says, "A is for Andrew" or reacts to seeing his name, we can show him that letters make that word. I have worked with two-year-old children who show no interest in their own names. They are not ready for letter names and sounds. It will happen. We need to keep trying and wait for it.

The foundation for literacy readiness lies in the unlikely places in our classrooms. The first steps to reading and writing come from the students' imaginations (Stone & Stone, n.d.). When children pretend to be mommy or daddy or a superhero or princess, they are embodying symbolism. They are literally standing in for someone else. They have to understand that one object can be a symbol for something else, because letters and words are symbols. Letters are shapes that symbolize sounds.

The letters themselves on a piece of paper have no sound. We attribute certain sounds to certain letters. Words are sounds that symbolize things, actions, and concepts. When we look at a foreign language, we don't know what it means because we don't know what the words are symbolizing. Dramatic playtime is essential for children to accept that one thing can be another. It is also where they become storytellers, and it is the first place where teachers can attach the word "story" to actions. When children are pretending, we need to talk to them about that pretend so that we understand their symbolism. We should never assume we are thinking what they are thinking. No two people have exactly the same worldview, and that is true of our students, too. Just because we were once young, it isn't true that they pretend or symbolize what we might imagine.

The blobs of paint on the easel paper and the scribbles done with markers are also literacy skills. Children need to strengthen the muscles in their arms and hands. They need to make large, sweeping motions on an easel to strengthen their gross motor muscles (Tavalieri & Schmakel, 2016). They make connections between the sections of the brain when their arms sweep from left to right, right to left, up and down, and back. When children sweep their arms from left to right, they are practicing the coordination in the brain that they will need to go back and forth on a page. The arts and crafts in our classrooms are about this development. It is less important that a child master drawing a particular item than that she has time allotted to drawing. The product is not actually the house drawn that day. The product is the letters she will write in the future because she spent so much time doing what adults dismiss as scribbling. The more scribbling the better.

Play-Doh should be out on a table every day. Kneading, pinching, ripping, and cutting Play-Doh develops hand muscles (Tavalieri & Schmakel, 2016). When I was a girl and took tennis lessons, we were required to strengthen our grips with gadgets that we squeezed in our fists. They had a spring for resistance so our hands would need to be strong to squeeze the two ends of the exerciser together. For young children with small hands, molding clay and Play-Doh provide a similar result. They are forced to squeeze and manipulate with their finger muscles. Using clay and Play-Doh has become such a staple in the preschool classroom that we forget to acknowledge and communicate its importance in writing readiness.

Cutting with scissors is not only a skill children need to develop for creating crafts when they go to kindergarten. It is a means for building fine motor muscles (Zachry, 2016). Combine cutting with scissors with clay and Play-Doh, and the children are coordinating and strengthening their hands. Very inexpensive scissors may not cut paper well, but they do cut Play-Doh. Every Play-Doh station should have scissors as well as the custom-made rollers and molds.

If we examine the alphabet, we can see the individual figures and shapes that children need to be able to draw without assistance. Letters are made of lines—vertical, horizontal, and lines that cross each other. Letters have curves and dips. They have sharp corners. It is interesting that when you do an Internet search of the required pre-writing shapes, different sites have slightly different lists. All the lists, however, include the straight, curved, and crossing lines in some format. When children in our toddler classrooms first begin to draw independently, we can observe them drawing with curved lines and rounded corners. It is exciting when at some point, as they head toward or are in the pre-kindergarten year, we see them draw shapes with sharp corners. A triangle with sharp corners is cause for celebration. It means that the student will be able to write so many letters with more success and less critique. The child who can draw a triangle without assistance will not struggle to write A, V, M, N, and many other letters. Students who are still curving corners will struggle to accurately write letters, and therefore are not yet ready for formal writing lessons and expectations. The students who are curving corners should be welcome to pick up a pencil and try if they so desire, but mastery cannot be expected yet. We want early writing to be an exercise in their abilities and not in their inabilities. Until they can swiftly change direction when writing, we cannot expect anything near mastery of writing.

Our time on the playground exercising our large muscle groups is also pre-literacy skill development. Do you remember being in physical education class as a young child and having to do windmills? Windmills were that exercise during which we had to, in rapid succession, touch our right hand to our left foot, and then our left hand to our right foot. Windmills are tough, and gym students wonder when they will end. They served a very useful purpose, as do many of our exercises as young people. During windmills, we were creating pathways and connecting different parts of the brain. Those gym teachers were actually exercising our brains! Children who are climbing ladders, throwing balls, and running are building their brains as well as their bodies. It is essential that young children participate in activities during which they have to cross the midline of their bodies, developing gross motor skills.

During the preschool day, students should participate in both structured and unstructured gross motor play. Unstructured play is the time when they make the rules and the decisions. They pick the hula hoops or the slide. They choose to play with the ball, climb, or dig. Structured time is teacher directed. We might teach them to play red light, green light or organize a game of catch. By having a mix of structured and unstructured time, students get choice while at other times they are learning to follow directions and the rules of a game. By ensuring an equal amount of structured, teacher-led activities, we can ensure that students are exercising a variety of gross motor, fine motor, and coordination skills. If we only let them freely choose activities on the playground, they will often pick only the same activities because they are familiar or easy for them. The children who find going down the slide to be easy will head right for the slide. The students who have mastered catching a ball will want to play ball.

When I was in high school, I had already developed a pretty strong aversion to gym class. I wanted to get a good grade so that gym didn't keep me from qualifying for honor roll. I was gleeful when our school started to offer yoga. I knew I would be more successful than I was when attempting softball, and I would likely be injured less often than in a sport like volleyball. I chose yoga for as many marking periods as was allowed. I've seen young children do the same. When always given the choice of gross motor play, they pick that which they know they can do. Watch the children who are at ages when they are becoming more aware of their abilities and the abilities of their classmates. If they have trouble catching a ball, they will make themselves busy doing something else on the playground. They need adults to provide structure for part of the time so they are exposed to and attempting a variety of physical activities. We want to be very intentional in developing all the pre-literacy muscles and skills.

Teachers are tasked with not only helping students to develop a list of skills but also with doing it in such a way that the children are interested, engaged, and love learning. Watch young children when they are not engaged. They look away. They find any reason to go do something more exciting. When older students are bored, they ask to go to the restroom or for a drink of water. When younger students are bored, they simply disengage.

We need them to be interested in alphabet and the written word. We have to address the children based upon what interests them most. They are, as we have seen, egocentric, and so what interests them most is themselves. Their own drawing and writing are far more interesting to them than the drawings and writings of other people. Think of it like vacation pictures. You could look at your own vacation pictures more than once but no one wants to sit through scads of pictures of someone else's vacation. The young students are enamored with their own creations, so we need to develop the love of literacy, starting with their own work.

Given the opportunity and positive feedback, children can make amazing things. It has been years since I purchased an alphabet chart for an early childhood classroom of children ages three and up. The students create their own. All you need are inexpensive, large index cards, and markers. It is an unrealistic expectation that children ages three to five will master alphabet writing, so we need to be clear on the purpose of the exercise. Students create alphabet charts to be exposed to letters and beginning sounds while making a classroom display. On each index card, the teacher should write one letter of the alphabet in upper- and lower-case. The students get to decide whether they will pick a letter or name a word and are asked to illustrate the card. One student, for example, might say, "I want to draw Mommy." The teacher would give that student the Mm card, discuss the sound of Mm, write "Mommy" at the bottom, and ask the student to draw Mommy. Another student might say, "I want A." In that case, the teacher would tell the student the sound of A so they could decide on a word for the card together. Once again, the teacher would write the word on the bottom of the card and ask the student to illustrate. The alphabet could be completed over weeks and, when finally done, become a display of their work. Every year, we laminate the cards in one long and wide piece so it creates a wall hanging like a quilt. We put the letter cards in order and hang our alphabet quilt at a height that the students can walk up to it. They are always proud of their contributions to the class alphabet chart. They even start to teach each other. They will tell a classmate, "That's my mommy," and even if they don't say that it starts with M, the M is right there on the card. They visually connect the spoken word with the written word. They see the words and the letters. They never get tired of going up to that chart to see their drawings. When I show this to teachers during presentations, they ask what happens if a child picks a letter that has already been done. The teacher tells that child, "That letter is already done. Let's pick another one." The alphabet and word lesson becomes a lesson in functioning as part of a group. Sometimes, we all don't get exactly what we want.

When making the cards for the alphabet chart, the teacher will take dictation. The student will say, "I want to draw a lion," and the teacher will write "lion" on the card. Teachers also often take dictation when they ask students about their pieces of art. "What is that?" is a common question when getting ready to send art home. The teacher writes on the art so the parents will know that their child painted a house or drew a flower. Our use of dictation needs to be expanded as a means of demonstrating that the written word is the spoken word, and as a tool for creating a love of literature. Opportunities for taking dictation cross the curriculum and enable us to connect many different concepts. This models later learning when older students have to write about their science lab, answer open-ended questions, and write on particular themes.

Teachers can take dictation as soon as children become verbal. What students say needs to be put on paper throughout the preschool years. Eventually, students will see writing as a natural extension of thought and speaking.

Journaling shouldn't be restricted to older children. Journals can be created through dictation from the time children are saying one word at a time. Explain to students that a journal is whatever they want to say. The teacher should explain that she will write down exactly what they say—no editing. The purpose of the exercise is to show that the spoken word is made of letters and we can write what we say. Precise grammar can come later.

Add to their vocabulary by telling children they will be authors and illustrators. Authors write words and illustrators draw pictures. "Illustrate" should be an everyday word for preschoolers. They spend so much time illustrating! On paper that has lines to ensure neatness and a large square or rectangle to frame an illustration, write whatever the children say. Date each page and put them in inexpensive page protectors in a binder.

The journals make lovely keepsakes for parents at the end of the year. They are what their children said when they were in preschool. Teachers may choose to add pages to the journal weekly. Don't be surprised if students, particularly those in the pre-kindergarten year, ask to add to their journals more often. Rarely, in my experience, will a student want to add just one page per day. One sentence or thought goes on a page, and they have so much more than that to say once they get started. Each journal should have the student's name on the spine of the binder and be placed on a shelf where the children can easily reach them. When the journals are available, they are often selected by students for oral reading more often than published books.

Another shelf might contain books that the class has dictated during science experiments. Science shouldn't be an activity during which children just look and then walk away to play with something else. Deeper learning is encouraged when more time is taken to consider what the children are seeing, hearing, smelling, touching, and/or tasting. Those "findings" can be recorded in science books. A favorite preschool science activity is watching caterpillars turn into butterflies. Each year, students who observe the metamorphosis can record their observations by creating a class book about butterflies. Every step of the way, from caterpillar to chrysalis and cocoon to butterfly, the children can describe what they see for dictation and they can illustrate. Ideally, every student gets a page about each stage. The class butterfly book can have chapters such as "The Caterpillar Is . . ." and "The Cocoon Is . . ." Each student would have the chance to describe what he or she has observed and can contribute a page to the chapter in the class book. This project becomes their first experience with chapter books, and they are the authors!

There is no limit to the number of typical preschool activities that can become more child-centered and more play-like. Children learn best through play, so the more fun, the better. When we teach beginning sounds, we tend to tell children what begins with a sound, ask them to come up with words that start with a sound, or show them pictures. The pictures are usually wonderfully drawn illustrations in books or on cards. Never underestimate your ability to draw well enough for a preschooler to identify it.

For years, I have introduced letters and their sounds with a game of "guess what I drew." I am certainly not an artist. I never really progressed much past a preschool ability for drawing myself. That's the fun of the game. Draw while the students are in the room. After playing the game a few times, they will understand the routine and go to where the teacher is drawing. They enjoy guessing games and revel in guessing correctly. They look forward to this game. The children will begin to gather around a teacher who is drawing to try to guess the pictures before the game has really begun. Preschoolers are fantastic at identifying rudimentary drawings. Draw anything with wheels and children will start shouting, "Bus! Car! Truck!" and anything else they can think of with wheels. Draw a squiggly line with eyes and they yell, "Snake! Worm! Caterpillar!" They are bound to hit upon the actual answer. If they don't, hint. They enjoy hinting games, too. I remember one day when I drew what I thought was a reasonable horse. The children in the class guessed every four-legged animal but horse. When we got down to animals that I was amazed they knew, I realized my simple horse was not obvious to them. I said, "It has a mane. It has a tail." When they guessed unicorn, I had to give the most obvious hint, "It says neigh." They all declared, "Horse!" I wrote the word to show them H, wrote the lower- and uppercase forms of the letter, and reviewed the beginning sound of horse. As soon as I was done, a student said, "It looks like a unicorn without the horn." Another child said, "Unicorns aren't real." Several students argued that they are, and the lesson took an interesting and unexpected turn. That's early childhood education!

CHAPTER 10 QUICK NOTES

Literacy development begins in the less obvious classroom activities.

- Understanding symbolism starts with dramatic play. Just as a letter symbolizes a sound and words symbolize things or experiences, children who are pretending are experimenting with one object standing for another.

- Easel painting, playing with Play-Doh, and other art experiences build fine motor muscles and cross-lateral brain connections.
- Drawing enables us to see if children can form lines, corners, and other shapes needed to write letters successfully.
- Playground time and gross motor activities encourage brain connections.
- Develop a love of literacy by having students create the items in your classroom such as alphabet charts, dictated journals, and student-created books.
- Literacy activities should cross all curricular subjects.

CONVERSATION POINTS WHEN COMMUNICATING WITH PARENTS

- Teach parents that everything that children do is part of literacy skill development.
- Teach parents a variety of ways to encourage children to enjoy literacy skills that do not include the use of paper and pencils.
- Explain to parents that children imitate adults, so they need to see their adults reading and writing. If they only see adults on computers, they do not know that we value work on paper.

CHAPTER **11**

Realistic Expectations of Ourselves: Creating a Mindful Plan

When your business is human beings, anything can happen. Every day in an early childhood classroom may be thoughtfully prepared. There are lesson plans and activities staged for the arrival of the children, but rare is the day that goes as planned. The students are learning and need much guidance when interacting socially. They argue with each other. They run, jump, and fall. Perhaps one child gets sick and another writes all over himself with marker. It's a typical day filled with the unexpected. Many an early childhood teacher has wished for more eyes to watch them, more hands to reach everyone, and faster feet to get there before the falling child hits the ground. We cannot grow extra limbs, but we can learn to be reflective and intentional rather than reactive.

In order to be role models of coping and demonstrate appropriate behavior, teachers need to stop spending their days putting out fires. Embrace action rather than constant reaction. When we spend our days turning from one emergency to another, not only don't we accomplish what we intended but it is completely exhausting. People can only spend a limited amount of time feeling like they are chasing one problem after another before they become discouraged.

When I first began my career in early childhood, I worked in a toddler room. There isn't a busier place in an early childhood center. There is a curriculum of art, pre-literacy, science, music, self-help, and more to accomplish. There are diapers to change every two hours like clockwork. There is snack to distribute while we teach how to sit in a chair and eat at a table rather than graze at will. There were 15 toddlers to sunscreen, get snow clothes on, and convince to nap. In the toddler room, there is mayhem and there should be. These young children have just discovered that they can explore, and they do—all over, and never in the same direction. I was younger, but I remember being exhausted at the end of the day. Just the perpetual lifting onto the changing table was taxing, never mind the rest of the active day. At some point, I realized that I could arrive ready to do battle or I could arrive with reasonable goals and plans. I had my lesson plans well ahead of time. That wasn't the problem. I needed to have a plan to teach sitting at the table, standing in something almost like a line, coming to me when I called their names, and using their hands for a plethora of activities instead of pushing and hitting. The list of what they needed to learn to function as any kind of group seemed endless and daunting. It was so many years ago, in that toddler room, that I started to develop an understanding of the power of reflection and intention. I started to distinguish what was possible from what was not, as well as what was a priority and what was not.

I realized that planning to teach it all at once wasn't realistic. It was a wish. Wishing doesn't stop when we become adults. Just as children cannot differentiate reality and fantasy, adults cannot always separate reality from wishes. I wished that through the magic of my instructions, they would all start sitting at the table. I wished that they would suddenly understand the gravity that adults attach to walking in a straight line. I wished they would learn so many things. One amazing day, I would walk into the classroom and they would be students. That would be the day that unicorns roamed the earth, a pot of gold was actually at the end of the rainbow, and birds whispered to us like cartoon characters. It was a lovely scene that would never happen. It is not how children learn and develop, and I cannot force their learning to happen differently. I knew that I had to plan for who they were and not who I needed them to be.

During every facet of our lives, we have a choice of being active or reactive, forging ahead without insight, or being reflective. Planning cannot start and end with a lesson plan book. Just as deeper learning cannot take place in a 10-minute segment of a preschool day, planning for meaningful days takes time and intention. It is not an early educator's job to survive the crises. It is an early educator's job to be ahead of the crises as often as possible. We should not be behind the proverbial eight ball all the time. We should be thinking two to three moves ahead of that eight ball.

Schools have missions and goals for their institution. The school's mission and goals are general statements that do not address individuality of children. It is the teacher's job to address the individuality in the class. Go from reactive to intentional by setting additional goals that relate to each human being in your classroom. Spend the first few weeks observing the children. Ask yourself:

- Who is each child and what needs does that child bring to your classroom?
- What strengths, what gifts, does each child bring to the world that can enhance the environment?

We have a very human tendency to observe for the negative. One child may be observed using his hands to communicate through shoving and hitting. Another child may be observed climbing rather than keeping her feet on the ground. Some children will be academically ahead of the bell curve of developmental range, and others will be behind. Every single child brings skills to be learned and skills already mastered. Each and every child also brings gifts to the world. Our observations need to be about how the children complement each other. We need to observe based on our curiosity about human nature and a desire to facilitate behavioral and academic learning.

Stand in the middle of the chaos of your classroom and start to plan. Determine what goals you have socially, communally, and individually for the social and behavioral growth of the children in that room. What developmentally appropriate and reality based skills do you want the children to have realistically learned before leaving at the end of the school year?

I enjoy asking kindergarten teachers what skills they appreciate seeing in their incoming students. Many kindergarten teachers have told me that they would like the children to be able to put on their own coats, zip them, put on their own shoes, use the bathroom properly, and open their own lunch containers. They appreciate getting a class with children who have had positive social interaction and understand that hands are not for hitting. They understand that not all their new students will have mastered oral vs. physical communication and some of the self-help skills. They do know that some children entering kindergarten can write and are beginning readers and others are not. They will take that from there.

Your goal list might include sitting while eating instead of taking a bite and leaving the table. It might include asking to go to the bathroom. It will most likely include teaching children strategies for when they are frustrated. A list of goals is just a start, but it is a start that has to be honed and crafted carefully. Write your list of goals. Walk away from it. Keep watching the children. Go back to the list and honestly cross out all the wishes that are not anchored in the reality of the age group or the dynamic of the current class.

A list of goals is where many adults begin and end planning. The goals are just the beginning of becoming more focused and intentional. Goals need to be prioritized and dissected. First, each teacher needs to decide the order of importance. We cannot wave a wand and improve everything at once. Put your goals on index cards or in your computer on a list that you can cut and paste. What goals are immediate? The answer should always be that the immediate goals address health and safety. Which of them is the most important? That becomes Action Item A.

Action Item A needs dissection, and all the goals will require the same exercise. We need to specifically name the Action Item. It cannot be vague, as in "Less chaos." It needs to be specific—"Less running in the classroom," for example. Running is a health and safety concern. Walking rather than running in a classroom is a learned skill that is appropriate for preschoolers. The goal—less running where the children can get hurt—needs to be broken down into teachable segments and tools.

To deconstruct a goal and become intentional rather than reactionary, we need to ask ourselves several questions:

1. What behavior do I want to teach instead of this behavior?
2. What are the specific steps to teaching it?
3. How can I acknowledge success?
4. When do I consider this skill mastered?

Remember that we cannot change a behavior or stop a behavior without replacing it. When behavior is inappropriate, ask yourself: "What can I tell the child to do in place of the behavior?" In the case of running, the simple answer is walking. When the goal is to get everyone to line up when requested, the answer isn't as clear cut. Specifically, do the students need to line up in a particular order or place? Is the goal to teach the children to stand without touching each other? The goal might also be to teach the children to wait near the door for the teacher rather than opening the door and leaving before the adult is ready to go. For use of the bathroom, the first priority can be asking to go, while in another classroom the priority may be pulling up pants independently. If students are wearing clothes that impede independence, the first step in proactively achieving the goal may be to contact parents to explain the importance of child-friendly bathroom clothing. Each teacher has to determine the replacement action for his or her classroom.

In one class in my school, the children were new to eating lunch in a classroom. They had much to learn. The goal for the staff was to improve lunchtime self-help skills. The Action Items were to teach the three-year-olds to:

1. Stay seated while eating.
2. Open containers and ask for help when not possible.
3. Eat as well as talk.
4. Clean up by throwing out garbage and putting reusable containers back in lunch bags.
5. Zip up lunch bags with used containers.
6. Put lunch bags by the classroom door.

The teacher had to determine her priorities. Lunch would happen no matter the order of priority of Action Items, so she decided that staying seated was Action Item 1.

Once teachers have decided on the list of specific Action Items and their order of priority, the task becomes to determine how it can be taught to children who have agendas of their own. What are we replacing the behavior with, and how? In this example, the teacher wanted to replace leaving the table while eating with staying at the table, but she knew that the children had to be intrigued by the concept. If they don't care, it's much harder, if not entirely impossible, to have a lasting lesson.

Children watch everything we do and try to do the same in their pretend worlds. Adults need to both verbally encourage wanted actions and demonstrate them. In our lunchtime scenario, this was a challenge. The teacher wanted them to sit, but she cannot. She realistically has to open containers, get forks or spoons if needed, and respond to other requests. I offered to help and to figure out a way that melded what three-year-olds value and want to emulate with the very mundane task of sitting while eating.

On day one of teaching about staying at the table, I brought my lunch into the classroom. In other settings it might be feasible for a teacher assistant to open lunches while the teacher commits to staying at the table or vice-versa. I asked the students if I could eat with them. One sweet girl said, "Sure!" I told them that I was going to stay in my chair the whole time we ate. I said, "I am going to tough it out. I know it's hard but we are strong and brave and we can do it." Young children love to pretend to be strong and brave like superheroes, rescue workers, princes, princesses, and even their very strong and brave parents or grandparents. They could relate to strong and brave and embrace it as a goal for themselves. I said, "Let's tough it out together like heroes. We can do it!" They liked this game. I did not move from my seat once. I reminded them when needed and, even when not, I pointed out how strong and brave they were being. I did exactly the same on day two. On the third day, I was unfortunately detained in a meeting. I went to the classroom as soon as I could and apologized to the students and teacher. She told me not to worry. The students were great during snack and lunch. One of the boys looked at his classmates at the beginning of snack and said, "Okay, we are toughing it out," and they did. I wasn't needed anymore. Mission accomplished.

To be completely honest, it wasn't entirely mission accomplished because we had more Action Items for our lunchtime goal. It was time to go back to the list. As each Action Item is accomplished, physically perform an action that crosses it out. Cross it out with a pen. Delete it from your computerized list. A feeling of mastering steps is good for everyone.

Determine the next priority in your Action Items. Consider the steps you will take to demonstrate the wanted skill and reinforce it. Often in early childhood classrooms, we forget that some children don't learn best from oral commands. The deconstruction of your Action Items may include not only demonstration but verbal as well as visual reinforcement. When the children accomplish a task, take a picture. When a child who is usually climbing on the furniture has her feet on the ground, take a picture. It is a visual depiction of doing the right thing. When the child climbs again, you can show her own image and ask, "Where were your feet when we took this? See, they were on the floor. Feet go on the floor just like on this day."

At some point during the lunchtime goal process, the classroom teacher decided that putting lunch boxes by the door was the Action Item to be focused on. All but one of the students put the lunch box at the door. One student left it on the table every day and ran to play. He didn't like leaving play to put his lunch box in the right place. The lesson needed to be positively taught so a power struggle wouldn't ensue. Action Items should be encouraged in a way that does not set up battle lines.

At the end of lunch when I was in the classroom, I did observe the dilemma. There was nothing compelling about putting his lunch box with the others. The train table was far more interesting. The teacher needed to make a game of putting the lunch boxes together. She needed to find a way to make that mundane task feel compelling. She told the students that if they all put their lunch boxes in place, the class would get to play their favorite game with the beanbag. She reminded them that the beanbag game would only take place if they all put lunch boxes in place, and they should remind each other to do so. The first time the boy walked away from the table without complying, the teacher said, "Uh-oh—what does he need to do?"

The children started proclaiming, "Your lunch box! Get your lunch box!"

The teacher made a game of getting him and racing back to the table. The children all laughed. It became routine to remind him about placing his lunchbox. The goal was met when he started to place it in the correct place without the teacher's help.

The successes need to be acknowledged and celebrated. To a young child, jumping up and down while high-fiving and saying, "Yay!" is celebration. No balloons, confetti, or parades are needed. On that first day when our student brought his lunch box to the door without a teacher, we celebrated. I went over to him and told him that he should be proud of himself. We high-fived. We thumbs-upped. We were all smiles.

We were celebrating the one success, but we understood that a skill is not mastered until it happens repeatedly. We didn't know if we had witnessed a one-time event. That skill was considered mastered when he zipped his bag and brought it to the door almost every day. When he was distracted by the sight of the train table and needed reminding, he did come back with us to accomplish the task. When the reminder was only needed on occasion, the teacher moved on to another goal. Only the staff in that room who wanted to create a more conducive eating environment could determine the definition of mastery. They were realistic. They knew the children would have their own priorities that would sometimes distract them. Being proactive is not synonymous with demanding perfection. Perfection is a wish. It is not real.

Realistically speaking, we need to try to teach skills that we believe are within the capability of our students. Sometimes, we are right about their capabilities and sometimes we are not. There are some goals that need to be revisited after a few months of additional growth. Likewise, there are times when we will carefully outline Action Items and discover that they are working for some students but not all. We will need to rethink our approach.

Schools have a life. They are morphing, changing environments that require us to change with them. When we sit in June and look at pictures of our students in their first days with us in September, we are astonished at how much they have grown. They are taller. They look a bit older. They have changed right in front of us. We cannot demand that they grow to their June height in September. It just happens in its own good time, and their parents have to adjust by buying new clothes. In preschool classrooms, a child who was easy to lift in September may not be so portable in June. We adjust to that physical change. When the child becomes heavy and we want to comfort her, we sit and gather her in our arms rather than lift. We purposefully change our approach. Our approach and methodology for being proactive has to change as they change emotionally and grow socially. It has to change as they acquire new skills, one at a time. Our September goals may not relate at all to our June goals. We need to be flexible and know that just because it is written does not mean it is permanently etched in stone.

I once had a conversation with a teacher of three-year-olds that has stayed with me for years. The teacher was trying to teach her students to sit together for meals. For one student, being with his classmates during meals was easy, but sitting—well, sitting was another matter. He needed to stand. He expressed his discomfort in the chair by squirming, sliding, standing, and sitting over and over. He was in perpetual motion in that chair. The teacher was dismayed. She said to me, "He can't."

I said, "That's right. He can't."

She repeated, "He can't."

I repeated, "Correct. He can't." This conversation was obviously going nowhere fast. I added, "So if we both know he can't, now what?"

The teacher said, "I might have to let him stand."

I said, "Yes, he might be better off standing. We now know that is the case for many older students, so why not him?"

She offered the student the choice—sit nicely in the chair or stand. He chose stand. He stayed by the table and ate well while standing. That was in October. By March, the teacher noticed that he seemed better able to sit for periods of time. She tried again by offering the choice—sit or stand. He chose sitting and, while he still needed reminders, he proved that children change and grow and our goals and expectations need to do the same for every individual.

Becoming more reflective and proactive rather than reactionary can become a habit. It can become how you approach every student, every class, every year. Before your year starts—or if it already has then before next week or next month starts—begin reflecting. At the end of every day, consider what went well and what you would like to accomplish. Be prepared to change that list as you learn more about the children in your class and as they mature. Remember, just because they can't today doesn't mean they never will.

CHAPTER 11 QUICK NOTES

- Embrace action rather than constant reaction.
- Plan for who the students are rather than who you wish they would be.
- Set goals that are for the actual individuals in your class, not just for the class or the school as a whole.
- Write a list of goals. Watch the children. Revise the list based on honest observation of their abilities.
- Put goals on index cards so they can be reordered.
- For every action item, ask yourself:

  1. What behavior do I want to teach instead of this behavior?
  2. What are the specific steps to teaching it?
  3. How can I acknowledge success?
  4. When do I consider this skill mastered?

CONVERSATION POINTS WHEN COMMUNICATING WITH PARENTS

- Teach parents about being intentional and the role that intentionality plays in working with young children.
- Explain your goals to parents. Sharing your goals helps parents to see your journey with their children and highlights the learning that doesn't appear on paper.

CHAPTER 12

Parent Education About Appropriate Practice: How to Ease Their Fears

There are many buzz phrases in early childhood education. We tell parents that children learn through play. We talk about developmentally appropriate practice. We explain to worried parents that children aren't "ready yet" or that skills "will come as the child develops." Phrases, buzzwords, and assurances do little to ease the fears of parents. Early childhood educators need to accept two roles—that of teaching children and of teaching parents. To help our early learners, we need to teach parents about a time that they only have vague memories of and have difficulty understanding. Adults are egocentric in their own way. They see the world from an adult point of view, where progress is marked by products rather than process. Early childhood professionals need to strive to improve our communication about how children learn.

Parents tend to be very interested in pre-literacy and pre-math skills. They want to be sure that their children are being readied to read and to calculate. Early childhood educators understand that nearly every activity is a pre-literacy and/or pre-math skill builder. Doing a puzzle helps to hone fine motor skills and coordination while it promotes the development of problem-solving skills. Using Play-Doh strengthens hand muscles. Building with blocks is intrinsic learning about weight, balance, size, and geometry. Pretending is the first understanding of symbolism. We need to consistently communicate with parents about the skills that children learn during what looks, to an adult, like meaningless playtime. Playtime is brain development time. It is problem solving time and critical thinking time.

We cannot expect parents to understand how and what children learn when we keep it a secret. We don't share our knowledge enough, and we communicate about it in preschool-level words. If we want to be respected as professionals, we need to represent what we do in a professional manner. That means using the big words.

I've had the experience of spending a whole day with preschoolers, going home, and speaking to my family as if they were those preschoolers. We need to consciously adjust our intellectual level for our audience. "They had a great time today," needs to become "They honed their critical thinking skills today, and that will serve them well when they are asked to analyze reading in the future." Likewise, "The students were so cute when they pretended to be their parents today," needs to become "The students were pretending to be their parents, which is the beginning of an understanding of symbolism. When the students pretend, they discover that one thing can stand in the place of another—just like a letter is a shape that stands in the place of a sound, and words symbolize things in the world. They need to pretend to begin that understanding of the abstract nature of language."

For everything the students do in your classroom, there are multiple skills being honed. We need to report this learning as often as we tend to report what our students are eating or how often they use the bathroom. Reports that simply say, "Becky enjoyed the puzzles today" tell nothing of importance. Parents are living in a world of immediate results. They can reach into their pockets, pull out their smartphones, and learn anything. They wait for nothing. Information, communication, and news are literally at their fingertips. It is natural that for many people, waiting is nothing but an annoyance. They want results now. It isn't an attack on educators that expectations have become a demand for immediate gratification. It is simply a reflection of the society in which we live. If parents want learning results to happen faster than children develop, then we need to explain better how we are encouraging that development.

In a typical early childhood classroom, students engage in a variety of activities each day. Each day, at least one of the activities needs to be explained to parents in terms of skill building. The communication can be in a variety of formats. Sometimes, you may want to send an email with a long explanation and provide pictures of activities that took place. You may decide to send a detailed monthly newsletter. On a day-to-day basis, pictures of activities or student-created art or writing can be hung in the hallway with a brief list of what skills were honed during the activity.

Create a "Did you know . . .?" document for communicating early childhood learning facts to parents. Along with pictures of students building, participating in science activities, using Play-Doh, painting at an easel and more, hang signs:

- Did you know . . . Children who are playing dress-up are also participating in a pre-literacy activity? A letter is a symbol for a sound. A word is a symbol for things in the world. Your child is learning symbolism by being someone else!
- Did you know . . . Children who make choices and decisions and explore are becoming critical thinkers? Critical thinking skills aid in comprehension, math, and other subjects. Critical thinking can be taught!
- Did you know . . . Building with blocks is a geometry and math skill builder? Your child is learning about balance, weight, measurements, physics—they just can't tell you that!

- Did you know . . . Painting at the easel is a pre-writing skill builder? Your child is developing the muscles in the hands and arms that are needed to hold the pencil correctly.

"Did you know" notices, signs, and emails should be a constant refrain during the preschool year. The truth is that they do not know. They cannot connect the blobs of paint on the easel paper to future sentence writing unless we make that connection for them. We are educated in methodology, and we forget that parents are not. We have unrealistic expectations of the parents and their knowledge of early childhood learning. If you are unsure of the reasons for activities, do some research. It's important for all adults to understand how preschool activities connect to learning and development.

Along with information about the academics that so worry parents, we need to be sure to communicate information about social and emotional development. Some parents worry when their children struggle with separation anxiety, and others worry when they don't. All parents need to learn that while it is hard to leave a crying child, it is an opportunity for their children to learn that they can survive without constant parental intervention. Separation anxiety is normal. That is a sentence too few parents hear. In their quest for an always-happy childhood, the parents of children with separation anxiety wish for a day when their child will go smiling and bounding into the classroom; yet, the parents whose children don't cry at separation worry that their children don't miss them. Another important lesson for parents is that their children do miss them. Rare is the young child who never mentions loved ones. Even if children don't use the sentence, "I miss my mother," they draw their parents or pretend to be their parents.

We need to teach parents about emotional intelligence. They need to be reminded that emotions are normal, whether pleasant or unpleasant. Everyone is scared sometimes or sad sometimes or hesitant sometimes.

The parents need to learn that we are here to teach coping skills and not the eradication of emotions.

Parents desperately want their children to not only be happy at every moment, but to be popular. They want them to play with other children all the time. That is not reality, but the parents do not understand why their children don't interact all the time. It is important to send information home about the stages of play. The information that we know about how children play and the different types of play should be shared. We participate in the overemphasis of literacy skills when the only information we communicate relates to reading and writing. Send home articles, newsletters, and emails about the importance of coping skills, the types of socialization, and the ways to teach self-help skills.

Just as children who are visual learners should be shown pictures of themselves going through the daily routine, picking up toys from the floor, sitting for mealtimes, and other activities that we wish to teach children, parents need to be shown pictures of their children learning these skills. Seek written permission for photography. Explain to parents that, with written permission, you can give them glimpses into their children's day, the skills being learned, and the routine that is being followed. We can tell parents, "We offer your children a chance to write," but they feel so much better when a picture in an email or in the hallway depicts the children writing. Use those pictures to point out the subtle skills. A picture of children writing, for example, could be captioned with the phrase, "Pencil holding practice." Not every bit of writing is about copying letters and numbers, after all. A picture of students at the easel can be described with the phrase, "Strengthening our fine motor muscles in our hands." There is always more to pictures of children in preschool than meets the eye. When I read a biography, I enjoy looking at the pictures of the people leading their lives. Similarly, parents will appreciate your narrative about child development being sprinkled with pictures of their children in real time.

"Did you know" messages help to educate and share our knowledge. "Do you remember" messages are equally if not more powerful. Throughout the preschool year and in all different formats, invite parents to remember. Remember the smell of clay and the feel of finger paint. Remember the mysteries that you explored in your yard. Remember the feeling of swinging higher and higher while you tried to swing so high that you would flip over the bar. Remember how much we learned by playing with our neighbors without adults immediately nearby to intervene. The parents have forgotten lying in the grass and marveling at the ants marching in formation. They are attending to important business, and they don't take time to consider how much they learned by making ramps for their toy cars.

They also do not or choose not to remember how it felt when they could not please a parent, a grandparent, or a teacher. They don't remember the terrible feeling of never being good enough. They need to recall how maddening it was to have their own emotions treated as if they weren't valid or to be constantly pulled out of their social comfort zone. Their own childhoods, all of our childhoods, include a plethora of experiences that should inform their treatment of their own children. When you have parents gathered, remind them. Explain that you will not make their children feel that terrible, self-defeating feeling of trying to please people who can never be pleased.

Ask the parents to think, look back, and tell you the feelings from childhood that they both want their children to experience and about the feelings that they prefer their children not have to endure if possible. Remind the parents that children need to figure out how their actions, and their words impact others, and we are here to help explain it to them.

We want their children to revel in the warmth of the sun on a chilly day while we take 15 minutes away from the desks to feel the weather that matches new vocabulary words. We have the ability to teach the magic of learning by being encouraging when their children try, and we have the knowledge to support their children when they are learning coping mechanisms. Relate it to their own struggles as young children so they will be more apt to remember that their children are complex self-discoverers, just as they once were years ago.

In addition to sending communication home, we need to invite the parents into our school settings. Open-door policies, mandated in many states, should be advertised to parents who are enrolled in your preschool. Even in states with mandatory open-door policies, parents may ask for permission to come to the classroom for special celebrations. Having the policy is different than throwing our doors wide open. When preschools put an open-door policy in a handbook but never mention it, the impression is that you don't really embrace it. Parents need to know that they are welcome in the classrooms at any time, because after all we have nothing to hide. In fact, we have a lot of information to share.

Not only are we willing to share our days with them, parents need to know that we respect their role as the primary experts on their own children. Children do not only learn socialization, emotional intelligence, and academics within our four walls. That learning should be seamless between home and school. We help to make the connection between home and school more fluid when we let parents know that they are more than welcome anytime. It is sometimes advisable to wait while students adjust to a new teacher, a new school year, or other change in the preschool day. Then, come anytime.

When parents do come for an open-door policy visit, narrate your room. Grasp the opportunity to give a tour of the students' work and art. Show the parents the pictures you display of children going through their days. Explain the educational importance of everything in the room, from the blocks to the dress-up outfits to the goldfish in the bowl. Your classrooms may look like their vision of early childhood, but that doesn't mean that parents understand why everything they expect to see is actually in the space.

Add to your open-door policy by planning adult visitation days. Invite parents, grandparents, or other adults who are important people in the students' lives to come to your classroom and experience preschool. While it is important that the adults hear about your days, it makes it even more relevant when they experience them. Plan a couple of days in your year when parents come to the class to be preschool students. Rather than observe, they should be immersed in the preschool activities.

Tell the parents that they will be treated like preschoolers. Have the adults participate in your messiest art project, your most sensory science experiments, and the silliest educational songs. While they are painting their hands and digging into the mud, explain the importance of multi-sensory activities. Not only will parents have a hands-on "how and why we do what we do" experience, the students will so thoroughly enjoy watching their loved ones learn about a routine that they are now expert in. Early childhood students can feel so proud as they help their parents to find the puzzles or spread the finger paint or learn the words to a familiar song. Their adults will get a firsthand view of how much the children have learned to do independently. Everyone wins, everyone learns about each other, when we spend a day in each other's world. Take-your-child-to-work days were started to show children what it is like to be their parents—where they go, who they see, and what it is like to have a job. Take-your-adult-to-preschool is equally important and teaches the same lessons.

Setting up a partnership with parents—sharing our knowledge and professionalism, respecting their knowledge about their children, and communicating about best practices—helps to lay a foundation for more difficult conversations. We would be remiss if we did not approach parents with our observations of behaviors that need to be addressed or skills that need remediation. It isn't easy to have to go to a parent to inform them of a possible need for evaluation for therapies and extra help. It also isn't easy for parents to hear that you are concerned about skill development.

We need to remember that whenever we speak to parents about their children, we are talking about their babies. These children whom we have watched grow so much is so few years are still babies. Most human parents spend 18 or more years teaching their children to be independent while ever so slowly letting go of our dreams for them as they develop their own lives. When we go to a two-, three-, or four-year-old's parents with a developmental issue, we are asking them to let go of dreams so very soon. Some of them cannot. They are not ready.

Early childhood professionals need to respect the parents' emotions as well as the emotions of their children. The parents have a right to hope and dream. It is our job to inform. It is not our job to destroy people. It is frustrating when we know that a child can be helped so much from some occupational or physical therapy and the parents refuse to seek it. We get upset, because when all else is stripped away, we want what we see the best for the students in our care. We are not, however, their parents and ultimately those are not our decisions to make. Just as we respect the parents who seek evaluation and help, we need to respect those who do not. The goal of having open communication with parents should include all parents, those who are ready to hear us and those who are not. Just because they aren't ready to hear us doesn't mean we have to shut the door to all communication. There are other things they can learn from us about early childhood education, and there are still things we can learn about their children from them.

There is a familiarity from seeing people every day that can take away from our viewpoint of each other as having valuable information to share. Teachers often chuckle when I tell them that the parents in my center know that I write and speak, but they really listen to experts from outside my school. When you are their own person, the one they see all the time, they don't view you the same way as a visiting presenter. Bemoaning the fact that familiarity seems to eradicate the knowledge you have gained over the years doesn't change the situation. We need to focus on what parents need to know rather than our own egos. Bring experts into your school to parent meetings. The importance of transmitting information about what is developmentally appropriate and what are reasonable expectations of young children needs to outweigh our desire to be the person teaching it. You are, in fact, communicating with parents when you invite them to a presentation or to a documentary. Just as children need multiple forms of delivery of information, so do their parents. The words may not be coming from you, but the event did. Just once per year, plan for a speaker, or a film, about how young children learn.

Ultimately, every communication with parents should be aimed at easing their fears. In order to address their fears, we have to identify and define them. Their fears are not personal attacks on our abilities. We need to remove ourselves from the emotions and address the facts. Parents are worried that in this highly competitive world, their children will not succeed. Parents are concerned that lack of socialization skills will equate to emotional issues. They watch the news and they see all the reports about teen depression, eating disorders, self-mutilation behaviors, and more. They don't want that for their children so they need to learn how to foster confidence and self-worth. Some behaviors are biologically based, but we can teach parents to be as supportive as possible. They know that jobs are hard to come by, and even getting into college is difficult. We can teach them that pushing their children before they are developmentally ready for concepts does not guarantee future success. It is our job to teach everyone—children and parents—that providing a foundation based in appropriate expectations, acceptance of individuality, and encouragement of independent thinking is what points a child toward a positive experience as the years go by.

ACKNOWLEDGMENTS

Educating doesn't happen alone in a vacuum, and neither does writing a book about educating. I have been fortunate to have had my life touched by so many children, parents, colleagues, and mentors. All along my life journey, I have learned from each one of you and I am so grateful.

Specifically, in relation to this book, I need to thank the parents and staff who gave permission for their stories to be told and their pictures to bring life to the pages. While I promised not to use names of minors or their location, I know that Gale Conti, Sheila Gold, Lisa Reingold, Bari Aronson, and Marcie Levitt won't mind seeing their names in print. Thank you for your encouragement during this project.

I also need to thank the people who said or did things that made me say, "That would be great in my book!" Thanks to everyone who granted permission to tell your stories, and the many others whose lives touched mine during my journey in this field.

Along the way, I have received priceless advice from generous people. Thank you, Linda Bozzo, for offering your insights and answering my questions about all that comes with being an author. We met long before either of us were authors and now we share this unique experience. I'm grateful to be able to lunch and chat with someone who knows. I would be remiss if I did not thank Jackie Held. When I was incredulous at the gift of this opportunity and slightly terrified by it, Jackie said, "With your feet firmly on the ground and your arms wide open, embrace the experience." You might not remember saying that sentence but I have repeated it to myself often during this process.

Before I wrote this book, I didn't even know that beta readers existed or that one of the best was a colleague. Thank you, Janis Knight, for offering your time and for the detailed notes from this little-known and best-kept secret talent of yours.

I am ever grateful to everyone at W.W. Norton & Company who participated in the process that made this book a reality. I will forever remember the moment when I read Deborah Malmud's email asking if I ever considered writing a book. I am humbled by your belief that I had something to say that mattered, and I appreciate all your efforts more than I can express.

Over the years, my family has in some ways given more to this career than I have myself. Working full time, consulting and speaking, and adding a book project to my responsibilities has been the equivalent of working two and a half or more full-time jobs. When something had to give, my family always willingly did. Weeks would go by without seeing my mother Gail Maloff or communicating with my sisters and friends because I've been so busy. Thank you for understanding the increase in text messages and lack of time face to face. I also am ever grateful for the encouragement that my uncle Howard Feldman offered during this process. When I told him that this book was becoming reality, he said, "You will be immortal now." Your love of reading, admiration of authors, and support have been priceless to me and helped me to become not only a voracious reader but a humbled author.

My two children, Michael and Scott Terebush, grew up with a busy working mom who did her best to juggle it all. They are now wonderful young adults who make me proud and who talk about how unhappy I would have been if I didn't have a career of my own. The fact that they understand me so well and that they are supportive made taking the time to write this possible. I may thrive from this work, but you both are the reason that my life has such meaning.

Last but most definitely not least, accurate words don't even exist to thank my husband Todd Terebush. We met when I was 19 years old and he was on the brink of turning 20. We have experienced it all together—glorious and tragic, daily wins, and struggles. I am the luckiest woman in the world because when I wanted to pursue this crazy and time-consuming career, he simply picked up at home where I left off. We have always been 50-50 partners, but adding this book to my responsibilities tipped the already out-of-balance scale. When I doubt, he says, "You can do this." When I am speaking, he is in the audience whenever possible. When I succeed, he rejoices with me. The best decision I ever made was returning your "Hello" at that college party with a smile and "Hi." Our children have the best father, and I have been blessed with you in my life.

RECOMMENDED READING

Are you interested in learning more about how children think and learn? Here are some of my favorites:

Vivian Gussin Paley's *You Can't Say You Can't Play* is an all time favorite. All Books by Vivian Gussin Paley are important reading for early educators, and include:

- *Bad Guys Don't Have Birthdays: Fantasy Play at Four* (1988)
- *You Can't Say You Can't Play* (1993)
- *The Girl With the Brown Crayon* (1997)
- *The Kindness of Children* (1999)
- *A Child's Work: The Importance of Fantasy Play* (2004)
- *The Boy on the Beach: Building Community through Play* (2010)
- *Boys and Girls: Superheroes in the Doll Corner* (New Edition, 2014)

The National Association for the Education of Young Children (NAEYC) offers both magazines and books. I recommend looking at their materials about developmentally appropriate practice, effective circle time, and more, at naeyc.org.

I also enjoy learning about how we think and learn. To learn more about questioning, read *A More Beautiful Question: The Power of Inquiry to Spark Breakthrough Ideas* (2014) by Warren Berger.

If you enjoy watching videos, look for interviews and materials from Bev Bos, who was a giant in the early childhood world and is sorely missed.

REFERENCES

12 Life Lessons from Mister Rogers. (n.d.). Retrieved from: http://parade.com/379451/hthompson/12-life-lessons-from-mister-rogers

American Academy of Pediatrics. (2014). *Bring out the best in your children.* Retrieved from: https://www.aap.org/en-us/Documents/ttb_bring_out_best.pdf

Arnsten, A. (2009). Stress signalling pathways that impair prefrontal cortex structure and function. *Nature Reviews Neuroscience 10*(6): 410–422.

Berger, W. (2014). *A More Beautiful Question: The Power of Inquiry to Spark Breakthrough Ideas.* New York: Bloomsbury.

Bodrova, E., Germcroth, C., and Leong, D. (2013). Play and self-regulation: Lessons from Vygotsky. *American Journal of Play 6*(1): 112–115.

Center for Science & Law. (2012). *Prefrontal Cortex Dysfunction and Impulsivity.* Retrieved from: www.neulaw.org/blog/1034-class-blog/3898-prefrontal-cortex-dysfunction-and-impulsivity

Child Development Institute. (n.d.). *Is Your Child Achieving Milestones in the Developmental Sequence?* Retrieved from: http://childdevelopmentinfo.com/child-development/devsequence

CIRCKLES MOTIVITY: *An Introvert's Brain vs an Extrovert's Brain.* (n.d.). Retrieved from http://circkles.com/motivity/motivityarchive2014/Motivitysept14.php

Emotional Intelligence. *Psychology Today.* (n.d.). Retrieved from: www.psychologytoday.com/basics/emotional-intelligence

Erikson, E. H. (1950). *Childhood and Society*. New York: W.W. Norton & Company.

Friedman, W. J. (2000). The development of children's knowledge of the times of future events. *Child Development 71*(4), 913–932. doi:10.1111/1467-8624.00199

Harms, T., Clifford, R. M., and Cryer, D.. *Early Childhood Environment Rating Scale*. 3rd ed. New York: Teachers College Press, 2004.

K12 Academics. *History of Preschool in the United States* (n.d.). Retrieved from http://www.k12academics.com/systems-formal-education/preschool-education/history-preschool-united-states#.Vqzp8rIrLIU

Kim, S. and Lee, D. (2011). Prefrontal cortex dysfunction and impulsivity. *Biological Psychiatry 69*(12): 1140–1146.

Laking, P. (2001). In: M. E. Hertzig & E. A. Farmer (Eds.). *Annual Progress in Child Psychiatry and Child Development 1998*. Philadelphia: Bruner/Mazel, 1999. *Child Psychology and Psychiatry Review 6*(03). doi:10.1017/s1360641701302691

Lillard, A., Lerner, M., Hopkins, E., Dore, R., Smith, E., and Palmquist, C. (2012). The impact of pretend play on children's development: A review of the evidence. *Psychological Bulletin 1*(34), 2–3.

McLeod, S. (2013). Psychosocial Stages. *Erik Erikson: Simply Psychology*. Retrieved from https://www.scribd.com/document/174877910/Erik-Erikson-Psychosocial-Stages-Simply-Psychology

McLeod, S. A. (2015). Preoperational Stage. Retrieved from www.simplypsychology.org/preoperational.html

National Institute for Play. (n.d.). *Pattern of Play*. Retrieved from: www.nifplay.org/science/pattern-play

National Institutes of Health. (2005). *NIH News in Health*. Retrieved from: https://newsinhealth.nih.gov/2005/september2005/docs/01features_02.htm

Parten, M. B. (1932). Social participation among pre-school children. *The*

Journal of Abnormal and Social Psychology 27(3), 243–269. doi:10.1037/h0074524

Piaget, Jean. (1997) *The Moral Judgment of the Child.* New York: Simon & Schuster.

School Sparks. (2016). *Gross Motor Development.* Retrieved from: http://www.schoolsparks.com/early-childhood-development/gross-motor

Sharon, T., & Woolley, J. D. (2004). Do monsters dream? Young children's understanding of the fantasy/reality distinction. *British Journal of Developmental Psychology* 22(2), 293–310.

Stone, S. J. and Stone, W. (n.d.). Symbolic play and emergent literacy. n. pag. International Council for Children's Play. Retrieved from: www.iccp-play.org/documents/brno/stone1.pdf

The American Institute of Stress. (n.d.). *Take a Deep Breath.* Retrieved from: www.stress.org/take-a-deep-breath

Tavalieri, D. and Schmakel, G. (n.d.). Building Gross and Fine Motor Skills in Children. The Family Center. Retrieved from: www.familycenterweb.org/index.php/ask-the-experts/28-asktheexpertscategory/186-building-gross-and-fine-motor-skills-in-children

Waters, Frances S. (2016) *Healing the fractured child: diagnosis and treatment of youth with dissociation.* New York: Springer Publishing Company.

Whetnall, E. M. (1933). The Moral Judgment of the Child. By Jean Piaget. (International Library of Psychology and Philosophy. London: Kegan Paul, Trench, Trübner & Co. 1932.

Yeager, D. S. and Dweck, C. S. (2012). Mindsets that promote resilience: When students believe that personal characteristics can be developed. *Educational Psychologist,* 47(4), 302–314. doi:10.1080/00461520.2012.722805

Zachry, A. (n.d.). Teaching preschoolers to use scissors. Retrieved from: http://www.parents.com/toddlers-preschoolers/development/physical/teaching-preschoolers-to-use-scissors

INDEX